Advanced Reviews for *Just the Way He Walked*

Just the Way He Walked is a moving testimonial of a mother's undying love and dedication to her son as he falls into addiction following the divorce of his parents. This memoir is a great lesson for all who are living the nightmare of an addicted loved one.

—Susan G. Weidener, author of *Again in a Heartbeat, A Memoir of Love, Loss and Dating Again.*

Just the Way He Walked is a very powerful memoir giving hope to parents/caregivers everywhere who struggle with the question, "How can I help my alcoholic son/daughter?"

—Dorit Sasson, Certified SEO Coach, content strategist and author of Accidental Soldier.

. . . a beautifully written, deeply insightful and candid account of the effects of addiction on entire families. This story that spans decades is also a tribute to faith that can lend hope to any family dealing with the addiction of loved ones.

—Sharon Lippincott, author of *The Heart and Craft of Memoir Writing*

*In *Just the Way He Walked*, Kathleen Pooler has painted a masterful portrait of addiction and codependency. Anyone who loves an addict will recognize this story. A memoir that is both heartbreaking and uplifting.

—Lynne M. Spreen, author of the *Karen Grace/ Blues Series.*

Kathleen Pooler's sensitive and articulate description of the heartache of addiction moved me deeply. To have struggled through the addiction of your son and had the diagnosis of cancer at the same time . . . her courage and determination will be a tremendous inspiration to many.

—Charlene D. Jones, M.Ed/M.A Meditation Teacher, Psychotherapist and author of *The Stain: A Book of Reincarnation, Karma & the Release From Suffering* and *Medicine Buddha/Medicine Mind.*

The deeper I read into Kathy's story, the more I wanted to cry out to God, "How much should one person have to endure?" Battling Stage Four Non-Hodgkin's Lymphoma, for decades she also agonized over her son's drug and alcohol abuse. Kathy's unfailing love for her son prompted everything she did to help him, yet he kept having relapses. Often driven to despair, she didn't understand that her enabling hindered him from taking responsibility for his actions and choices. She wrote, "It would take years and many Al-Anon meetings and prayers for me to break my addiction to his addiction and be able to set firm boundaries for myself and him." Throughout it all, Kathy never stopped loving her son, always had hope for him and for herself, and always trusted God. Because her heart's desire is to offer hope to those dealing with addictions, Kathy offers a wealth of materials at the end of her memoir. They include sixteen lessons she learned over twenty-three years, several pages of resources for parents of addicted children, and book discussion questions.

—Linda K. Thomas, memoir teacher and author of *Grandma's Letter s From Africa* and *Please God, Don't Make Me Go.*

If family alcoholism and the author's physical illnesses were this story's only focus, readers would miss the pot of gold at the end—a rainbow of hope, one metaphor in Kathy Pooler's excellent memoir, *Just the Way He Walked.*

Though no sunshiny fairy tale, Kathy's courageous story takes the reader through the ugly to reveal the beautiful, reason enough to keep turning the pages in anticipation of a hopeful ending, as I did reading her fine sequel to *Ever Faithful to His Lead.*

—Marian Longenecker Beaman, author of *Mennonite Daughter: The Story of a Plain Girl.*

Kathy Pooler's new memoir, *Just The Way He Walked*, is truly a love story. It tells the harrowing story of a mother's love and never-ending concern for her alcohol addicted son, her own growing health problems, and her son's continuing alcoholism that started when he was a teenager. He finally listens to his mother's pleas to turn his life around when he was in his thirties, and he consents to let her publish this book so that it can be a help to others with alcoholism in their lives. That is his special gift in return for his mother's love.

—Madeline Sharples, author of *Leaving the Hall Light On and Papa's Shoes.*

Pooler's memoir is well written. Her story is written with others in mind trying to help a family member or friend struggling with addiction. Descriptions of her emotions are honest and painful for the reader. But, we must expect reality to shine through in a tough story such as this.

—Sherrey Meyer, Write and Blogger at *Life in the Slow Lane.*

Just the Way He Walked

Just the Way He Walked

A MOTHER'S STORY OF HEALING AND HOPE

KATHLEEN POOLER

Just the Way He Walked: A Mother's Story of Healing and Hope

For information about this title or to order other books and/or electronic media, contact the publisher:

Sunnyview Press
Niskayuna, New York
https://krpooler.com
kpooler63@gmail.com

Library of Congress Preassigned Control Number: 2019908552

ISBNs
Print: 978-1-7332253-0-4
eBook: 978-1-7332253-1-1

Printed in the United States of America

Cover and Interior design: 1106 Design

Author's Note

This is a true story reconstructed from memory. I have changed several names and identifying characteristics of some of the people and settings in this book to protect their privacy. These are my memories and may differ from others' memories of the same events.

I invite you to continue the conversation with me on my blog, *Memoir Writer's Journey* at https://krpooler.com. See "About the Author" for more social media connections.

Other Works

Synopsis for Ever Faithful to His Lead:
My Journey Away From Emotional Abuse

NOTHING CAN RESCUE HER UNTIL SHE DECIDES
TO RESCUE HERSELF

How does a young woman from a stable, loving family make so many wise choices when it comes to career, but so many poor choices when it comes to love?

Kathy must face her self-defeating patterns before she and her children become a statistic.

Her life and the lives of her two children depend upon the choices she makes, and the chances she takes.

Join Kathy on her roller-coaster ride of self-discovery, from shame and guilt to inner strength in her tears to triumph story.

Amazon Link: https://www.amazon.com/Ever-Faithful-His-Lead-Emotional-ebook/dp/B00M17OXYO

The Edge of Hope

It came without knocking. A wingless angel.
Silently, so silently she entered, like a thief in the dark
Dragging me into jagged, cavernous corners of despair.
I gifted my body to surgeons, wrapped in blue ribbon
To do as they pleased. Adorned in scrappy gowns, rainbow tubes,
Hole in my chest, black patches, tremors, I lay crumbled.
Thoughts of mother and father, eons departed, rushed in
Filling me with long-lost memories of happy times around the fire
Ludo, Snakes and Ladders, steaming mulligatawny soup.
Friends who span continents and time, locked in my heart,
Blew comfort, solace, hope with letters and cards that arrived
In the mail. Simple words to empower, bring gentleness, love.
Yet as my blood fermented and ravaged, I yearned for moments of stillness.
Stillness at the water's edge, blurred on a misty lake, forgetting
The present, envisioning a future with no pain, no punctures.
The years have skipped, bounded, galloped. I am here, breathing in warmth,
Exhaling light, with thoughts of mortality closer to the stars.
In the brilliant changing landscape, the caterpillar turns, hesitates, falls.
And suddenly I, the blue spirit butterfly, emerge radiant, triumphant,
Poised for takeoff.

~ By the late Cheryl Braganza, from *Cheryl Braganza: The Persistent Painter, Poet, Pianist*, January 2015.
Published with permission.

To My Children, Brian and Leigh Ann

For all you have endured, for the fine adults you have become, and for keeping hope alive in me. You are my joy.

Foreword

by Sandra Swenson

I don't remember exactly when I came to know Kathy, but it was at a time in my life that I will never forget. Struggling mightily to understand and cope with my son's addiction (while attempting to conquer it for him), I did what we moms so often do—I scoured the internet, searching for help and hope and a magic solution. It was during this time that I virtually met Kathy, whose path so closely mirrored mine. Not only were we both floundering around in the bewildering and scary world of our adult children's addictions, trying to figure out how to do the right thing even when we didn't know what the right thing was, we had also both taken up writing during the second half-century of our lives—not only to preserve our own sanity, but to share our stories so that other moms might feel less shame, less guilt, and less alone. Our connection was immediate; as is so often the case among moms with addicted children, we knew a deep understanding and empathy before the first word was even exchanged.

Kathy and I have clocked a lot of miles and years since our paths first crossed, and so, even though we've never met face-to-face, I know Kathy as a wise and comforting friend, a voice of courage and strength, and a fellow member of an ever-growing sisterhood—a true lifeline in this tragic reality we live.

There is great comfort, wisdom, hope and healing to be found in the awareness that someone else is living the same horror and heartache—but too often we moms suffer in silence. It takes courage to speak up, to share our stories with honesty and openness, but Kathy has done just that in *Just the Way He Walked.* Laced with faith and fear and fierce motherly love, her words open a window into the realities of loving a child suffering with the disease of addiction (and, in doing so, demonstrates to other moms why bringing the truths of addiction out of the shadows is so important).

Within the pages of *Just the Way He Walked*, Kathy explores the issues of wishful thinking, boundaries, family dynamics, enabling, and letting go. She takes us through the "clash of dreams and reality", the "agony of wishing for and waiting for someone else to change", the process of coming to terms with changing what she can, and the beauty of unconditional love.

I am honored to walk alongside Kathy as she helps other moms on this journey feel less shame, less guilt, and less alone. And I am grateful for her voice—for the strength and example she portrays in *Just the Way He Walked.*

Together we are stronger.

—Sandy Swenson
Author, Advocate and Power Mom

Author of *The Joey Song: A Mother's Story of Her Son's Addiction*; *Tending Dandelions: Honest Meditations for Mothers with Addicted Children*; *Readings for Moms of Addicts* app; and founder of www.MomPower.org.

Minneapolis, MN
2019

Acknowledgments

In the course of the twenty-some years it has taken me to write this story, my path has crossed with many supportive men and women who have accompanied me on my journey. In some cases, I have forgotten names but I will never forget the love and support offered me when I needed it the most.

To my memoir mentors from whom I learned the art and craft of memoir writing—Linda Joy Meyers, Susan Weidener, Denis Ledoux, Jerry Waxler, Sharon Lippincott and Maureen Murdock.

To my sisters at the International Women's Writing Guild who have guided me on my writing journey—Heather Cariou, Maureen Murdock, Susan Tiberghien, June Guild, Jan Phillips, Lisa Freedman, Marge Hahn. Thank you for lighting the path to my own creativity.

To my local writing group—Carol Bluestein, Julie Lomoe, Leslie Tabor, Judith Prest, Carol Marchewka, Leslie Neustadt—for your candid critique of my writing.

To my beta readers—Lynne Spreen, Sharon Lippincott, Christina Stark, Marian Beaman, Maureen Hand, Judith Prest, Charlene Jones, Janet Givens, Dorit Sasson, and Susan Weidener.

To professional developmental editors Dorit Sasson and Susan Weidener for their tireless efforts in helping me to shape my story and dig deeper into the narrative.

To the outstanding professionals at 1106 Book Design with Michelle DeFillippo, Brian Smith, Ronda Rawling and their editorial staff for helping me bring my story to life.

To my wonderful memoir community and blog followers for inspiring me every day. The list is exhaustive and if I start naming people, I fear I will leave someone out.

To my support community at Al-anon—Jeanie, Mary, Lisa, Judy and so many others. We shared our heartache and fears and together we survived one day at a time.

To the community of mothers of addicted children—Sandy Swenson, Libby Cataldi, D'Anne Burwell, Patty Welek Hall. We learn from one another's stories and together we are stronger.

To my faith community at Our Lady of Grace Catholic Church and Stephen's Catholic Church for your ongoing love and support through many trying times.

To my siblings—Tom, Gary, Paula—for their unwavering support throughout the years.

To the sweet memory of my beautiful parents—Robert and Kathryn Pease—for guiding me and helping me to find my way back home again.

To my children—Leigh Ann and Brian—for growing through the hardships and becoming responsible, beautiful adults. This story is my love letter to you both.

To my stepchildren—Rick, Shelley, Sarah and Ben—for loving me like a mother and for your ongoing support.

To my wonderful husband, Wayne for supporting me through the worst of times so we could experience the best of times together.

To my God who is the source of all good things. With Him, all things are possible.

Table of Contents

PART III: BREAKING THE CYCLE
(1999–2017)

PART ONE

Addiction Hits Home

Kathy and Brian, 1975

A mother clings to her baby boy, dreams of his future as he grows from cheerful cherub to rascally youth. Hope, like a butterfly, elusive and fleeting, floats in the air as the path leads to rugged terrain, steep and overwhelming.

~ Personal journal entry

PROLOGUE

A Mother Hopes, 2013

For twenty-three years, I feared my son Brian would die from his addiction to alcohol.

In October 2013, I attended a journaling workshop by The Women's Writing Circle in Philadelphia where I shared my story. Comforted by their care and concern, I broke twenty-three years of silence and pain to share my story of how I feared for my son's life due to his active drinking when the group was given a prompt. "If only . . ."—with the expectation that we would work in pairs and then share our responses with a bigger group of about twenty women. Shame threatened to overwhelm me.

Although Brian and I had spoken on the phone, I hadn't seen my thirty-eight-year-old son in eighteen months.

My heart pounded as soon as I began responding to the prompt. I was stepping into vulnerable territory; feelings of hope and heartache had flooded me ever since Brian had started drinking twenty-three years ago. Contrary to what I envisioned writing, I actually wrote and shared a letter to Brian, letting the women know that I would be, in fact, meeting him—for the first time in eighteen months, even though we had spoken on the phone—at Penn Station on my way back home.

Could I handle the emotions of sharing what felt like a very personal story with a wider audience? I didn't even know if he was okay. I wondered if I would feel confident enough talking to him about his drinking.

Dear Brian,

Sometimes I feel sad knowing you are still struggling with who you are and where you fit into the world. When I visualize you, I see your many talents.

I see the four-year-old boy who shared his dripping orange popsicle with his little friend Becky while the two of you sat at the end of the driveway one steamy summer afternoon.

I see the seven-year-old rascal at the top of the pine tree, waving your hands above your head, "Look, Ma. No hands!" as I watched in terror and frustration while trying to coax you down.

I see the kind, loving ten-year-old reaching out to hold the hand of an elderly nursing-home resident during a school field trip.

I look up at the gangly thirteen-year-old with the crackly voice before you dart off to joke and spar with your friends.

And I wonder: Where did it all go so wrong?

What happened to that son of mine who now sits in his apartment alone and struggles daily to make sense of the life he hasn't had? Who looks back at the lost opportunities and dreams and mourns his path?

With fierce mother love, I hang on to hope—hope that you will reconnect with that little boy within who has so much innate goodness and worth, hope that you will begin to see yourself as I see you—healthy, whole, and still filled with promise.

Love,
Mom

After reading my letter to the group, I looked up at their faces—full of consternation and engagement.

"You must read this letter to your son," one woman said, while several others nodded in agreement.

I felt hesitant. *What if he doesn't show? Will he be sober? Will he be open to what I have to say when I see him?*

Still undecided whether to read him the letter word for word, I encouraged myself to remain open to the possibility that he would show up at the station and that, at some point, I would open the letter.

When the one-day workshop was over, I boarded the Amtrak train the next day, relieved to find a window seat so I could be alone with my thoughts and take in the scenery. As I watched the skyline whizzing by, I reflected on how Brian would unravel me emotionally after each visit in times past. . . .

If you would have told me that the baby boy whose coal-dark eyes locked with mine would be lost to me and to himself for years on end, I would have scoffed at you. That little boy who looked for his Matchbox cars under the couch would grow up into a man still searching, only this time for his purpose and for the life he'd missed—the holidays when he was noticeably absent; the college opportunities that slipped away; the numerous jobs lost; his older sister, Leigh Ann's, missed wedding. On her wedding day in August of 2003, the lone, small, silver-framed place setting with his name on it was a grim reminder of the price he—and we, his family—had paid for his drinking.

Images of his own struggle, which he had shared with me whether he was sleep-deprived or hungry, had left me feeling emotionally unsettled after each visit. Each time, I'd ask myself, *Where is this son of mine, and why is he so lost in unknown places?*

But on this day, when I would soon see Brian for the first time in eighteen months, a faint glimmer of hope filled my heart. Maybe I'd taken in his absence as the new normal. Or maybe I had just shared my letter with a group of supportive female writers. Although his last major relapse had been in June 2012 and we had been in phone contact sporadically since then, the thought of peering into his dark eyes and the sensation of being wrapped in a warm hug energized me. Still, I couldn't help but worry. *Would he be clean and sober?*

I didn't know if my efforts in writing the letter would warrant the need to share my private thoughts with Brian. I didn't know if I would read him the letter I had written in the journaling workshop, but I decided to keep it handy, just in case I would break down. I'd learned not to ask Brian too many probing questions, so I wasn't sure what to expect. I even tried convincing myself that he was probably sober because he'd already committed to meeting me. But for the past twenty-three years, Brian's behavior had always been unpredictable. I could never trust in his decisions, and now I had to just live for the moment and hope everything was okay.

Contrary to what I'd expected, my train, due to arrive in New York City at three in the afternoon, arrived fifteen minutes early, leaving me with a feeling of dread. I recalled with alarm the times his drinking had taken precedence over his commitment to show up at family events, leaving me heartbroken. I pulled out the letter I had written just a few days before to ease my inner doubts. Reading my own words "with fierce mother love" gave me the inner strength I needed to fill myself with optimism and positivity until I'd finally see my son.

People rushed by me as I waited in the lobby. I saw a group of young adults huddled together laughing and hugging. I wanted to know Brian had good friends who truly cared about him. *How would he look? How would he be? Will his eyes be glassy and blood-shot?* I took a deep breath and visualized the clear-eyed, healthy son I had seen in the past. I kept reminding myself to hope that he was still there.

The crowd quickly dispersed, and I looked around the station, back and forth. Presently a young man emerged from the crowd; his shape looked familiar—broad shoulders, head bobbing high above the crowd. I clutched my chest and took a deep breath . . . it was just the way he walked.

CHAPTER 1

Moving On, 1990

In August of 1990, two angry teens and one guilt-ridden, exhausted single-again mother crammed into a 1986 cream-colored Ford Taurus, filled to the brim with suitcases, pillows, blankets, and Muffin, our long-haired yellow stray cat. We were bound for a new beginning after my second divorce from an abusive second husband who suffered from untreated bipolar disease. This move was my do-or-die moment. Leigh Ann, fifteen, and Brian, thirteen, would become more rooted, I thought, if they were near family by the time they were ready for college. My plan was to re-establish myself in my nursing career and create stability for all of us. I would start a job as Director of Nursing in Cobyville's community hospital. The guilt and shame of uprooting my children multiple times—of not providing them with a father—suffocated me. *Did I really think that this was all my fault?*

After leaving Trenton, Missouri, and traveling for eighteen hours over a three-day period, we arrived in Cobyville, a small town in eastern New York.

"At least we'll get to see Dad more, Leigh," Brian said.

I could see Leigh Ann through my rearview mirror. She stared out her window in stony silence, a grimace on her face.

"Don't count on it."

Although I had learned not to rely on Ed to be present for our children, I always held out hope that he would come around, especially if we lived closer to him—one of the reasons I decided to move back east.

Shortly after passing the sign for Cobyville, I turned up our new street, Pleasantview Avenue. Modest, neat homes with groomed lawns in a quiet neighborhood gave me a good feeling. Then I saw a small, white house with an attached garage. The bay window had a curtain off the rod, dangling like a white scarf on a stranded car along the highway. The lawn and bushes were overgrown.

"M-o-o-m, it looks like a drug house!" Leigh Ann and Brian yelled as I pulled into the driveway.

I couldn't disagree.

"Hey, relax," I said, in an attempt to reassure them—and myself. "Grandma will be here to help, and you both know how she loves to clean and rearrange other people's homes."

Mom had accompanied me on my many moves and found great pleasure from helping us get settled. When they were little and Grandma visited, the kids came home from school and rushed to their bedrooms to see what magic she had created for them, with new curtains, pictures on the wall, and colorful bedspreads.

These moves were wearing on me—this one was the fifth move in seven years. I was especially worried about Brian—a young man growing into manhood without the benefit of a steady father-figure. Before we left Missouri, I'd heard rumors that he'd been seen at parties with the older, drinking crowd. If it was true, I was glad to move and start fresh again.

I knew Brian missed his dad. My dad was always there for me. I remember one particular incident when I was fifteen. The bandleader had ridiculed me in front of the entire band. I hadn't heard what he said or why, but others told me. I went home for lunch and mentioned it to Dad because I was confused and hurt. He calmly rose from the table, walked over to the school one block away, and confronted the bandleader.

"You will never treat my daughter like that again. And furthermore, I expect you to apologize to her."

I knew what Brian was missing, and it shook me to the core.

As angry as I was at Ed for not fulfilling his role as a father, I knew the father-son bond was a tender one, a delicate balance I had to achieve to nurture the bond, even while being angry at Ed's absence.

One day before we left Missouri, I walked into my bedroom to get my contacts. The sheer curtain rippled through the air as Brian leaned forward in the corner chair. A quick glance reminded me that his thirteen-year-old body was changing before my eyes. His little-boy body had begun to sprout to my height, 5'7", filling in with expanding muscles and a crackly voice. He looked preoccupied.

"Hi, B. What's going on?"

"Oh, nothing," he said, pausing a moment while keeping his head down. "I was just thinking about Clint."

"What about Clint?"

"Clint's dad takes him fishing," he said, as he lowered his head into his hands and began sobbing. Wet tears streamed down his blotched face as he gasped in between sobs.

"I wish Dad could take me fishing."

The guilt for being so far away from Ed always seemed to linger at times like these, like an unwanted guest. I realized that no matter how far away we were, Ed would always be their dad and that Brian would long for him. No one could fill the deep longing in his heart.

Brian was a clone of his father, with his thick mop of brown hair and eyes that danced with mischief. By the time Brian started playing tee-ball at age five, he showed promise of following in his dad's footsteps as a star baseball player.

My children helped sustain my hope that they would thrive, despite Ed's drinking. When I left Ed back in 1977, I believed I was saving them from the heartache and chaos that addiction creates. I saw them watching their father lose himself to alcohol, envisioning them being embarrassed to bring their friends home for fear of what Ed would do when they got older.

Oh, how I ached for both my children that Ed could not be there for them in a way they needed and deserved. In later years, I ached for Ed and all he'd missed because of his drinking.

Being a single mom was not part of the dream. I felt flawed, incomplete. I was on-stage, playing a role, ill-prepared and resistant. I grew up in a loving, stable family. My parents rarely drank and were always there for me and my three siblings. My father was a prince—steady, wise, and devoted. My hero. Mom was the heart of our family, a doting Italian mother. Home was a secure, safe place. I was returning home again.

Kathy, Leigh Ann, and Brian, 1990, in Cobyville

I moved to Cobyville carrying my biggest fear in my heart. Though I still held out hope that being closer to Ed, who had stayed in Syracuse, would make a positive difference in our children's lives, I tried to stifle my biggest fear—of Brian repeating his father's cycle of alcohol abuse.

PART TWO

Dancing with the Devil and Other Such Things

I am the one who got caught up in the dance with the devil. I was ever hopeful that I would learn the steps that would sweep my son from the devil's clutches—only to be left in the dust of doubt and despair as I felt the beast stealing my son, robbing him of his life, his future.

I am the one who felt the grief and mourned my son, absent from my life, yet still alive somewhere beneath the chaos of addiction.

Oh, let me stop the dance, starve the beast!

But, how can I love my son while ignoring the addiction? There are three of us in this dance.

Let me be strong, like a dandelion, and endure—loving my son, hating his addiction.

Let me stop the dance.

~ Personal journal entry

CHAPTER 2

Addiction Pays a Visit, 1971–77

"M-o-o-m, quit worrying. I'll just be with Justin," he said, wiping his mouth with his hand after guzzling orange juice from the carton as we stood in our kitchen.

I stood face to face with my unpredictable son, who surpassed me in height, growing well beyond my 5'7" into a 5'10" bundle of boundless energy and slick banter.

"And 'Justin' is?" By then I was gripped with fear and anxiety and unraveling inside at the very thought of Brian not acting responsibly—of choosing the wrong friends, of drinking.

"He's one of the guys on the football team. You'll like him, Mom. He's cool," Brian said with ease.

"Friends are important, B," I said, "Pick them wisely, and be home by 6:00 p.m."

"A-OK. You know it, Mom."

He headed toward the door, turned, and nodded—as if to reassure me—and was gone.

I was on my way out to a barbecue with my new co-workers. I wanted to believe that he would be okay, but my insides stirred, and my mind raced. *Who is he meeting? Where will he be? This is his chance to start fresh, but will he?* I was fearful that he would choose the wrong crowd, as he had in Missouri.

I arrived at the barbecue an hour later but couldn't relax. Leigh Ann was with her new tennis teammates, Karen and Christy.

I could not shake the uneasy feeling of Brian repeating his father's pattern of heavy drinking and turning into someone I didn't care to be around. All kids experiment and test their limits, but this was different. I'd had a preview of what alcohol could and would do, and I knew there was a genetic predisposition to it. Ed was the "life of the party," whose drinking eventually led to DWI arrests, loss of jobs, loss of our marriage. And, ultimately, the loss of his health. I couldn't help but fixate on where drinking might lead Brian.

There seemed to be an unwritten rule: As much as Leigh Ann hated her brother's choice of friends and activities, she hesitated to talk to me about it. I was in the dark, a condition most likely reinforced by my own inability to face the truth of my son going down the wrong path. The thought of living with a son who abused alcohol terrified me. My anxious mind would not rest. Though I was acutely aware of the possibility, I was also fighting hard to deny it. It was too big to take in.

I carried these thoughts with me as I sat at the picnic table, trying to focus on the moment rather than obsess over my son's whereabouts.

Vern, my co-worker, joined me at the picnic table. "How are the kids adjusting?"

"Fine, as far as I know" I said. I wished I could believe my own words and was fearful that my negative thoughts would materialize if I acknowledged them.

"My kids, Mike and Dave, loved it here. They're both in college now, but they always want to come back for a visit," Vern said, adding, "Your kids will be fine, too."

I don't know why Vern's comment left me feeling so alone and fearful. I know he was only trying to reassure me that my kids would adjust to all the changes in their lives. Yet, my underlying lack of trust in Brian's ability to make the right choices of friends and activities made it difficult to separate out my imagined fears of Brian turning into his father with the reality before me—a teenager struggling to come of age in a new environment without the benefit of a male role model.

Are my fears justified? Am I overreacting? Were those tales from Missouri about drinking and stealing money true? Brian denied drinking and stealing money from his friends. Is he lying to me?

It was just the way he walked, with that self-assured, cocky stance that said he was in control. Or was it his ready smile and quick wit that reminded me of his father? Vern's comment made me realize that Brian was not just another normal kid, like Vern's kids were. He was Ed's son. It was just the way he walked.

"I hope you're right, Vern." I said, reeling myself back into the moment, appreciative of Vern's support.

The sun was warm and bright on that carefree late-summer day. Barely tinted leaves rustled in the soft breezes as Joyce brought the grilled hamburgers to the picnic table.

"Hot off the grill. Dig in," she said, rallying the group to gather around the table.

I fixed my plate in robot-style. *I'm not even hungry,* I thought. I remained worried about Brian's whereabouts while trying to stay focused on the conversation at hand.

"Hey, did you hear the story about . . ." my new boss Tim piped up, capturing the group's attention.

I decided to leave the party early, as Tim droned on about some little old lady who had tried to cut him off in traffic.

As I pulled into my driveway, my concerns about my children swirled in my head. I had a pretty good handle on Leigh Ann. Her friends were over a lot, and I was meeting some of their mothers. Little did I know that she was well on her way to becoming the "good sibling"—and maybe even the forgotten one—as she began to live in the oppressive shadow of her elusive, manipulative younger brother.

On the other hand, I had no handle on where Brian was or who his friends were, and I couldn't trust him, even for a second. I was getting an ominous feeling that he was befriending the "wrong crowd," even though I didn't really know for sure.

As I walked to the front door, I noticed how the bay window was neatly framed by crisp, white curtains and the lawn and bushes were trimmed. It was a sharp contrast to the first time the kids and I drove up to the house from Missouri.

I continued to the front door. The sweet odor of the newly mown lawn permeated the air. By all outward appearances, the house was settled. All was in order. I wanted to believe that this lived-in feeling could, in fact, be long-lasting.

I already felt hopelessly out of control when I thought of Brian and where he might be headed. I didn't know who he was with—let alone any phone numbers to call and find out.

As I turned the key and opened the door, a deafening silence engulfed me. I sat by the bay window and stared out at that sunny September day, hoping my mother's anxiety was unjustified. The curtains were not dangling anymore, but I was suspended in a weird state of pain and worry over some unknown as I dutifully watched and waited. A sense of helplessness washed over me. Being a single parent of two teenagers heightened my sense of loneliness. I felt like I was shivering on an iceberg in the middle of the ocean.

Alone and scared.

I walked into the kitchen to find Brian opening the door with more caution than seemed necessary.

"Hey, Mom—what's up?" he said, staring at me through hollow, glassy eyes as he swayed on unsteady feet.

The odor of stale alcohol sickened me. He stumbled, reeled, and fell on the floor at my feet as I looked on in horror and disbelief. His dark eyes, flashing and blazing, were fixed somewhere beyond me.

"Mommy, where is the *cah*?" said two-year-old Brian, looking up at me back in 1977, with his big cow eyes and full head of thick brown hair.

His Matchbox cars were lined up in front of the couch.

"Let's look under the couch."

Getting down on my hands and knees, I swept my hands into unknown territory as he waited expectantly. His dark eyes fixed on his mission, he left no doubt in my mind of the value of that one car. Every car was important in his world. When we went to the store to pick out another car, he scanned the collection of multi-colored vehicles with such intensity that I began to dread the task. I was always in a hurry, and Brian was on his own time. It was never a quick deal, so I definitely wanted to find that car. Stretching my arm under the couch, I retrieved a few plastic Legos, a rubber band, and a handful of dust balls in a futile attempt to rescue the only thing that mattered to him in his two-year-old mind. Back to the store to assuage his grief, his dark eyes, the window to his soul. It made me realize that each child is unique and that, as a mother, I needed to pay attention to my children's individual needs.

The chilling fact that I was looking at my drunk teenaged son shattered my vision of what I thought motherhood would be. I had dreamed of being married and having children since I was a young girl, playing with dolls in my bedroom. I hadn't factored in dealing with a wayward son.

A searing pain in its rawest form pierced me; my heart lodged in my throat, and my stomach churned. The panic tried to escape as I struggled to find my next breath. My insides screamed in terror.

No, Brian—not this! I cried to myself, but no words came, only a deep knowing that I was staring at my biggest fear. *I am mothering an addicted child.* Though I knew this was not just an isolated incident, I had yet to discover what this meant.

Brian stood up and meandered to his room. I stood in place for a moment, stunned as I watched him leave. Then I went to my bedroom and fell on my bed, fingering the tiny embossed flowers on my bedspread and waiting for the gush of tears that finally came.

Seeing Brian drunk for the first time propelled me into another dimension. I had seen Ed as I looked into Brian's distant eyes and watched him self-destruct. I danced around the reality in my own mind, wrestling my fears to the ground as I tried to hang on to the hope our son would outgrow this phase. It was all too real, and so was my helplessness and the gnawing desire to make it something it was not—just a normal stage to be resolved in time.

CHAPTER 3

Fear Takes the Lead, 1991

A few months later, in November, Brian stumbled into the kitchen after an evening out with his friends. Our eyes locked once again. His dreaded glassy stare made me feel helpless. I was swept up in the grief of watching my teenaged son slip away—like we were slowly descending into a giant sinkhole, an abyss, together. Immobilized.

In retrospect, I was denying my biggest fear, shoving it into the back corners of my mind, hoping it would go away. Magical thinking.

So, I did what I thought every responsible parent should do—I took on the responsibility for his behavior. I made excuses for school absences and brushed off a missing wine bottle or a steadily diminishing jar of quarters in my bedroom. After all, I was the one who had traipsed through Pennsylvania, Wisconsin, and Missouri with my children in hopes of finding a better life. I was always searching outside for the answer: that job, that location, that man who would make our lives better, while the real answers lay dormant inside me, untouched and untried—but, of course, I didn't realize that at the time.

For the last two years, when parenting Brian started to feel like a real struggle, I'd gone through the motions of parenting, floundering and stumbling along the way, never quite sure what I should or should not be doing. *What do I know about bringing up a boy?* I'd watched my mother and aunt struggle with rebellious sons—throwing their hands up in resignation and helplessness. Mom deferred to Dad, who, though normally laid back, would take the stairs two at a time, belt in hand, when provoked by my brother Tom. Although I never witnessed Dad actually using the belt, it seemed the mere suggestion of being whipped by a belt would alter Tom's behavior. Mom's sister, Aunt Rose, was a single parent with four boys, two of whom kept her wringing her hands and crying with their late-night escapades and scrapes with the law. I saw myself repeating this cycle of helplessness with Brian. The knowledge that my brothers and cousins had all turned out fine, despite their raucous beginnings, gave me the hope that Brian would make it through.

One Sunday afternoon in January 1991, five months after we moved, I heard an unexpected knock at the door. The basketball coach, Tim, was standing on the front porch, looking down at his feet as I opened the door. My fears were confirmed before he even opened his mouth.

"Brian's making a big mistake," he said as I invited him into the living room. He expressed concern about the crowd Brian was hanging around.

"I don't even know who these people are," I said, sighing deeply.

"Oh, they're just a group of townies who cause trouble with their drinking and partying."

"Brian has the talent. He could play and excel at any sport he participated in, but he's going down the wrong road," he said, adding, "I just wanted you to know my concerns."

"Thanks for letting me know," I said, though I really wanted to scream out, *What in the name of God am I supposed to do?*

The deep sorrow I felt was palpable as I watched the coach turn and walk out the door. I sank into the couch, pondering Brian's poor choices of friends that had kept resurfacing since the day we moved from Missouri. My fears for Brian's safety were confirmed with this visit and prompted a sense of urgency to take action, though I had yet to figure out what that would be. I replayed the tape in my mind of Brian's response when he was kicked off the football team the previous fall as a result of my own intervention with the coaches when I found out Brian had been drinking.

"Mom, all the kids drink, but their parents don't squeal on them."

"Brian, maybe you'll think twice before you drink again. There will be consequences," I said, adding, "Baseball season is approaching, and I'm sure you do not want to be kicked off the baseball team."

He glared and slammed the door behind him.

The expectation from the people I answered to—the hospital administrator and the hospital Board of Directors—that I maintain control in my job was very clear. It was up to me to set the boundaries.

As a single parent, I answered to no one but myself. I could call Ed on the phone and plead with him to step in. Ed had remarried, and he seemed to have settled down. But I anticipated he would not show up as he had proven to me often in the past, and, once again, I was left to go it alone.

Even though I had my reservations about Ed's commitment, I desperately needed his help with disciplining Brian, especially after we moved back to New York. Three months after coach Tim paid me a visit about Brian, he called me on the phone.

"I had to cut Brian from the basketball team."

I second-guessed my previous decision to report his drinking to the football coaches, and now, I was seeing the fallout. Sports had always been a healthy outlet for Brian and at least kept him physically active and occupied. I dreaded what would happen now, with all the extra time. I needed to hear coach Tim's rationale. *Maybe it was negotiable?* When I asked for his reasons, he said, resolutely,

"Brian's extracurricular activities would be a negative influence on the team. His attitude will spread to the rest of the guys." I wondered how Tim knew about Brian's activities. I assumed that living in a small town left no room for anonymity.

Ironic, I thought, *how Ed would chastise him about the very thing that had led to our divorce*. But, Ed was all we had, and I kept hoping even some contact with his father would be better than none. In my mind, Brian's relationship with his father was the key to his rebellious behavior and saving him from it. Several times, I pleaded with Ed on the phone,

"Ed, he's crying out for limits and fatherly guidance. He needs to see more of you."

"*Hmmph*. I'll see what I can do."

A few weeks later in 1991, I arrived home from a late-evening meeting at the hospital to find the shower curtain and rod dangling and a hole punched in the wall from a sibling scuffle.

"He's crazy!" Leigh Ann screamed. "I'm sick of him ruining my life!"

"She's a drama queen, Mom," Brian said in defense.

I stood there, trying to make sense of the chaos.

"What the heck happened that would cause this hole in the wall?"

Silence.

They both retreated to their bedrooms. I never got a clear-cut answer except I knew Brian had most likely antagonized his sister with his fits of anger and acting out.

My sense of control dwindled as my guilt for being away from home due to my job blossomed.

Years later, Leigh Ann would confess to me that she found her brother drunk and vomiting that night. "If I hadn't been there, he would have choked to death. I turned him onto his side and then helped him upstairs, where he began to punch the wall and rip the shower curtain from the rod. Mom, I saved his life." *Where was he getting the booze?* I didn't keep any in the house.

"Why didn't you tell me?" I said, horrified not only that Brian had almost died but also that Leigh Ann had stayed silent all those years.

"He made me promise not to tell," she said. "That's when I decided I wanted nothing to do with him. I felt so scared. I saw Dad when I looked at Brian that night."

This incident reminded me how Leigh Ann, from age three, had learned resilience from the moment she'd learned we'd be leaving Daddy.

"Is that because he's mean to you, Mommy?"

Wise beyond her years, she carried the burden of her perceptive nature. She developed an edginess as a teen that I would later recognize as a defense against her hurts and fears, but, at the time, this edginess stopped me in my tracks. It was hurtful, and I feared I was losing her, too. Her resilience taught me about persevering in hard times.

My intuition as a mother took over. I was terror-stricken for both my children. *How was I going to gain some control and save us all?*

Getting in touch with my intuition that day led me to take control of Brian's risky behavior right before baseball season just a few months later. I wrote up a baseball contract to regain some control and set up a meeting with his guidance counselor to discuss my concerns and review the contract I had written.

Mrs. Michael sat down at her desk and adjusted her glasses while she leaned in and read each line. She looked up after reading it, took her glasses off, and scowled,

"If you take something this important away from Brian, it may not have the results you are looking for."

I slumped back in my chair, like a deflated balloon, feeling a bit startled and confused by her statement.

"Really?" I said.

"Yes. If baseball is so important to him, and you take it away, he may rebel even more."

"Thanks. I'll give it more thought," I said, still feeling discouraged as I left her office and walked to my car.

By the time I turned into my driveway five minutes later, I decided to heed her advice: to forget the contract and let the events unfold naturally, even though I was disappointed that my well-intentioned efforts to regain some control had proven futile. Clearly, there had to be another way to take charge of this situation.

How I wished baseball was year-round! It could take my mind off reality for a while. When Brian earned a coveted position on the baseball varsity team along with two other freshmen, my heart filled with hope and optimism. Could it be that my son's involvement in baseball might even counteract his need to drink? Brian and his fellow-freshman team members John and Mike all excelled and were cited frequently in the daily newspaper for their notable achievements on the team. I reveled in the glow of Brian's success, particularly that he wasn't drinking—a taste of the way things used to be, a glimpse of how it could be.

Rays of sun streaked through the kitchen window one early July in 1991 as I read the morning's paper. School was out for the summer. As I scanned the front page, my eye caught Brian's picture in the sports section. My heart was pounding as I gazed in awe at the article naming him "Rookie of the Year" and a member of the county All-Star first team. My son—in the paper for his achievements! My heart soared with happiness and pride.

"Brian, get down here," I yelled from the bottom of the stairs.

"What, Mom?" he replied, rubbing his eyes as he stood in the doorway.

"Look." I raised my arm, waving the paper in front of him.

He lunged down the stairs, two steps at a time, took the paper from me, and shook his head to focus.

"Hey, how about that?" he said, blinking the sleep from his eyes.

"I'm so proud of you, B!" I said, hugging him as we swayed side to side in unison.

So maybe there *was* hope for him to completely turn around. For now, I just wanted to celebrate his success and envision Brian enjoying a normal life, staying involved with his friends, working hard at school, and staying out of trouble.

A month later, toward the end of summer vacation, we moved from our rented house with the cats—the first and only home we'd known since returning to New York State—to a large duplex on Main Street. The retired schoolteacher had returned from the Cape to reclaim her house. Brian and his friends helped with the move. But after the first load, Brian disappeared upstairs, where I found him sleeping while Simon, Jonathan, Ethan, and Don did most of the work. He was hung over—bloodshot eyes, sluggish, and lethargic. I dreaded the thought that it had all started again. His friends stayed on to finish bringing boxes in, shaking their heads and shrugging their shoulders.

Off and on over the summer, I discovered more evidence that Brian had been drinking—this time, empty beer cans stashed in the cellar—and with each incident, I sank deeper into helplessness and fear. Someone was supplying the beer, or he was stealing money to buy it. His friends started expressing concern about his drinking.

"He's not going to make it to twenty-five," his friend Don said.

I didn't ask about Brian—the truth is I didn't want to know—nor did his friends tell me what they knew about him, but all of us knew was that he was drinking again. In place of his energetic and cheerful self I had witnessed over the last few months, the other Brian was back—the one who sneered at me and his friends and punched walls and disappeared into the night, only to return many hours later.

Still, hope was the only way for me to make it through these wild days as I remembered his sports achievements from that previous summer. Deep inside, I was at a turning point. It was only a matter of time before I would have to seek out professional help for Brian. The question was: How would I go about doing that?

A few days after we moved to our new home on Main Street, Brian and I were invited to Don's house for a barbecue. Don's mom, Fran, and I had become friends. They lived on the outskirts of town, in the country, surrounded by trees and a stream that flowed through their backyard. The boys, Simon, Don, and Brian rolled up their pant legs and waded in the stream. Courtney, another classmate and friend, watched them wade as we sat together at the picnic table.

"Ya know, Brian told me when he made the varsity baseball team that he was gonna' get that "Red Bat" award for the highest batting average on the team," Courtney said, leaning toward me.

"Really?" Brian had earned this award in a school assembly at the end of the year for achieving a batting average of .488.

"Yep. And he really sounded determined," she nodded.

In the midst of the fear that addiction would take over his life, a fear that terrified me, I clung to any snippet of hope that Brian would be okay. I reminded myself of how Brian's determination was his saving grace, and he had the ability to overcome obstacles that his father, Ed, was not capable of doing.

For the next hour, he horsed around with Don and Simon. And for a few hours, I took a break from constant worry that consumed me around my son's risky behavior.

CHAPTER 4

Friday Night SOS Assignment, 1991

"What in the world are you still doing at 7:00 p.m.?" Fran asked, incredulous at the thought of anyone staying at work late on a Friday night. I had been named director of nursing of the 100-bed community hospital, and Fran had phoned me at work. Work had been my way of coping with the growing awareness that my son could be in trouble at any given moment.

Fran was also a single parent. Brian had told her I was always staying late at work, she shared. He was right.

There were enough issues that kept me at work every night, which meant I was constantly worried about not being at home for my kids. The medical staff was fighting the hospital administrator Tim, my boss. The doctors were loyal to a nearby hospital that wanted to take over management of our small facility, and Tim, hired by the same outside management company who had hired me, was fighting to stay independent. All the ingredients for warfare were in place. After only two months on the job, I was already beginning to experience battle fatigue.

During my first week of employment, at a medical staff meeting, I watched in horror as Tim, fifteen minutes into the meeting, stormed out of the boardroom, his dark, curly hair disheveled and brown eyes blazing. He and the Chief of Medicine, Dr. MacKay, had circled each other like a bullfighter and El Toro in the ring. Tim was the 250-pound bullfighter waving the red flag in front of him. Dr. MacKay was short in stature, with a slight build. He sat opposite Tim at the other end with his head down, tapping his pencil in rapid succession on the mahogany conference table like a bull would paw the ground in preparation for an attack. Every once in a while, he would shoot an angry glare at Tim.

In a matter of minutes, it became very clear that they hated each other. My first week, my first meeting on the job couldn't have been more uncomfortable. I nervously readjusted my position in the chair next to Tim. I was in the middle of a battle I didn't even understand. I had just moved eighteen hundred miles with two surly, resistant teens, and I was sitting in a room full of cranky, out-of-control toddlers disguised as grown men. The meeting broke up soon after Tim left, and I went into my office to call the recruiter who had placed me in the position.

"Pat, this is not getting off to a very good start," I said, right after the meeting, as I burst into tears of regret and dread. "What have I done?"

After filling her in on the meeting, she paused and then said, in her trademark calm, reassuring voice,

"I trust you will rise above it all, Kathy." She added, "Here's an opportunity to show what you're made of. Don't lower yourself to their level."

I held on to those words through each crisis and did the best I could to maintain control. Now, if I could only apply this to my home life . . .

Pat had become a caring friend over the past nine years of recruiting me. We first met back in 1984 in Spangler, Pennsylvania, where I had moved to from Syracuse for a Director of Nursing position in a small hospital. Six months after arriving with my two small children, I pondered my next move away from this small hospital embroiled in a pending nurses' strike. That led to Grove City, Pennsylvania, in 1984 and a progressive move to a larger hospital in another small town.

I had learned from those two previous positions that these types of behaviors were all part of small-town politics and that I'd better come up with a solid plan for surviving as the outsider. With a job to do and a family to support, there had to be a way to make the job work. Pat and I spoke on the phone frequently in the beginning, and, usually, by the time I hung up, I was calm enough to move on to the next crisis.

Fran's voice on the phone relieved me on that Friday night. Support both at work and at home felt scarce, as my sense of loneliness grew daily. It became evident that I needed to find my own support system to cope with the responsibilities at work and at home.

"You need to get a life, Kathy," she said.

"I'm listening," I said, nodding in agreement. It warmed me that Fran reached out to me in friendship.

"Leave right now, and go home and change," she said. "I'm going take you to a singles' dance."

"I don't want any part of that scene."

"Oh, it's not like that at all."

"Well, I'll think about it," I said.

"Besides, I'm really tired, and I'm worried about Brian."

Fran and I had discussed my concerns about Brian's drinking.

"He can hang out with Don." That made sense, since I knew he and Don were good friends.

Clearly, Fran was working hard at convincing me to get out, while I was making excuses why going wasn't a priority. I still had fresh wounds from my divorce from my second husband, Dan. Moving from Missouri did not take away the pain as quickly as I had hoped.

But after a few weeks, I finally gave in. Fran was right. I needed to get a life, and working late on a Friday was not going to be an option anymore. Fighting battles on both the home front and at work made me weary. I could use a break from Leigh Ann's icy stares, from Brian's lies about his whereabouts, and from the incessant bickering and game-playing at work. Not only were the doctors fighting Tim, but some of the long-term nurses were going to the board members with their complaints about staffing issues or pay rather than coming to me, which undermined my role and added to my stress level. The vulnerability of being new in town, holding a visible position as Director of Nursing at the local hospital, and going it alone converged to keep me on high alert. A break from all the tension at work and home sounded like a good idea.

A few weeks later, on a Friday, as I was getting ready to go with Fran to the dance, I felt queasy and awkward, like a young school girl getting ready for her first date. I'd been there so many times before. *Why did it always have to be so difficult to start over again?* I knew I deserved to find happiness, but I had a teenaged son and daughter who were struggling with the recent move. *Should I leave them for the evening? If I stayed home, they would be with their friends, and I'd be alone anyway.* I knew I had to start taking care of myself so that I could take better care of my children.

By the time Fran came to pick me up, I had told myself it was okay to go out, even though I had my doubts. I kept telling myself that Don was a good kid, and I talked myself into believing I could trust Brian would be safe if he hung out with him while I was gone.

But my anxiety increased with each mile we traveled during the forty-five-minute drive away from our small town. The drive into Albany was riddled with questions and uncertainties. Fran kept reassuring me by repeating that Don was aware of Brian's drinking problem and would watch him.

"Oh, Fran. What am I doing—going out at 9:00 p.m?"

"Just wait. You'll have fun," she said, her blue eyes sparkling, as she turned to look at me in the passenger seat.

"But I'm not ready to meet anyone." Fresh out of my second divorce, I didn't have much confidence in my ability to choose the right man to get involved with. *What impact would a new man have on my children, especially Brian?* And yet part of me wanted to be in a relationship, or I wouldn't be open to attending the dance. If I did meet someone I was attracted to, I knew I would need to take my time and proceed cautiously. Baby steps.

"Well, it's not like you have to marry the first person you dance with," she said, looking over at me and chuckling. I cringed at the thought of marriage.

Fran made me laugh at myself. She was tall, 5'10", and stately: a classic beauty with long blond hair that fell in soft curls around her oval face and high cheekbones. Her wide smile and sparkling blue eyes matched her outgoing personality. When she began talking, her Brooklyn accent left no doubt that she was a take-charge person.

I looked over at her as she drove and felt a gush of appreciation for how she had reached out to me. I had to give her credit for working so hard and for putting up with all my whining and insecurities. She made me feel safe, like she was a mentor in the fine art of socializing in the single-again world I was plunging back into.

Fran parked the car, and we walked into the Polish Community Center. I paused to take in a deep breath as Fran opened the door. I was walking into a new chapter in my life, and I had no idea what was in store. Tina Turner's "Proud Mary" blasted in the background, and men and women of varying ages milled around, laughing and talking. When we signed in at the front desk, Fran introduced me to Greg, the president of SOS (Singles Outreach Services). He had curly salt-and-pepper hair and horn-rimmed glasses. He greeted me with a warm smile and handshake.

"Welcome to SOS, Kathy," he said. "Hope you enjoy your evening."

Fran grabbed my arm and guided me into the dancehall. She led me through the crowd, introducing me to all her friends. It seemed everyone knew Fran, which reinforced my sense of security.

The sound of the music and Turner's belting voice soon melted my fears as I reconnected with what had always been my love of dancing. I stood at the edge of the dance floor and could barely contain myself from moving in rhythm to the music—Disco, Cha-Cha, Jitterbug, the Electric Slide. I couldn't remember the last time I had danced.

"Come on," Fran motioned, directing me to the front line next to her as the band played the Electric Slide. "Watch me."

She leaned forward and back, her blond curls flying in every direction as she shuffled and turned sharply. Soon, I was in unison with the crowd, laughing and falling into the groove as the lights flashed and the music blared. It warmed me up for the rest of the evening, and I danced every dance with a different partner each time.

They were nameless, faceless companions commissioned for the night to fulfill my dancing dreams, no strings attached. I twirled till I was dizzy to "Saturday Night Fever" with one partner and then moved on to do the salsa to "La Bamba" with someone else. I didn't care whom I danced with, nor did I want to get involved. By the end of the evening, I was drenched in sweat, but, like a runner at the end of a race, content. I looked at my watch and saw that it was 1:00 a.m. I was wide awake.

"Oh, sure," Fran said, teasing. "I work so hard dragging you, kicking and screaming, and you go off, a social butterfly—like it was your idea to begin with."

We stood on the nearly empty dance floor, bending over and laughing until we had to wipe the tears from our eyes. The band was packing up and walking past us as we made our way to the parking lot.

"As long as I can come and dance without getting involved with anyone, I'll be back," I said as the cold air blasted through the open door.

"Oh, really?" Fran said. "I knew you would like it once I got you here."

"I think it'll be my Friday night assignment from now on," I said, already looking forward to my return to the dance floor the following week.

The idea of having a brief reprieve from the battles that were raging around me made me smile when Fran suggested we come back next Friday night. I felt lighter and younger as I slid into the passenger seat of Fran's car. It was then I felt the familiar dread, wondering what I would find when I arrived home.

CHAPTER 5

Reality Sets In, 1991

Our new home on Main Street, a large, white, wood-framed duplex with a front porch, reminded me of Nan's home in Schenectady, New York, where I'd spent all my summers until I was seventeen years old. Memories of sitting under the peach tree while relatives swarmed my maternal grandmother's backyard on warm summer nights still wash over me like a soothing balm. The sweet taste of juice running down my chin from a peach I plucked off the tree still lingers today as I look back on that time. Now, here I was a single parent, dealing with a tough, demanding job and two recalcitrant and surly teens. As I looked around the large kitchen, I craved the return to the laughter and fun of those carefree summer days. The 1950-style Amana stove, side pantry, huge living room, dining room, and front porch brought Nan's presence into our new home. I was comforted to find a place that felt like home.

That night, as I pondered my life, I smelled the sweet aroma of the hyacinth bush beneath my bedroom window and felt in harmony with the soft breezes of the summer nights. Muffin, the long-haired yellow cat who adopted us right before we left Missouri, nestled peacefully at the end of my bed.

But, against this peaceful picture of being home again, a rapid, gushing river of doubt and fear about Brian's wayward path raged on, clashing with my longing and hope for a normal life. Within the first few months of our arrival in town, I had heard only snippets about the kids to avoid from the mothers of Brian's friends.

They were phantoms—fatherless boys who roamed the streets at night, failed in school, and were known to do drugs. I knew this because I heard loud knocks at my side door in early morning hours accompanied by hoots and hollers of Brian's name from a gang of them. I recognized their shapes as they vanished into the darkness. I didn't know names or faces, but I knew enough to feel anxious.

I knew I could always call Ed, but that didn't help much in the middle of the night when I lay awake, anxious and fretting over how to handle Brian. Panicked, I sat up in bed and tried to think of what I needed to do. The anger I felt toward Ed—an absent father both physically and emotionally to his son—added to my apprehension. But it only served to deplete me of the energy I needed to face the problem.

After a while, I realized that blaming Ed was getting me nowhere. My growing anger over Ed's lack of active participation in our children's lives had corroded into rage. I had carried that resentment with me since our 1977 divorce. I wanted to lift the burden off myself.

I felt the need to forgive Ed and move forward. The question was . . . how?

One night, after one of Brian's basketball games, Ed took Brian and me out to dinner at Fernando's, a local pub. Despite our differences, Ed and I had maintained a civil relationship since the divorce. Brian stepped away to visit with some friends as soon as Ed and I slipped into our booth.

Against the background of a boisterous bar crowd and John Denver's "Rocky Mountain High" on the jukebox, I looked across the booth at Ed as furls of smoke from the next booth swirled around his large frame. I started wringing my hands underneath the table and leaned forward,

"I want you to know, Ed, that I have forgiven you," I said, swallowing hard. "I want to set things straight so we can be there for our kids."

"Of course," Ed said, opening his eyes wide. He flashed a hint of a smile and nodded, "Thank you."

I exhaled slowly and nodded back at him.

He didn't ask any questions, nor did I offer any specifics, but somehow just addressing the fact that I was ready to let go of the burden of being angry with him consoled me.

I took a cleansing breath in and then slumped down a little in my seat, relieved but uncertain how this would make things better. We didn't talk further about specific plans on co-parenting, but I felt it was a start. Ed was not much of a talker. When we were married, he'd open up only after he drank. This time, Ed was sober. I felt it was an accomplishment to finally address his parenting, especially after all these years. I only hoped that he would rise to the challenges that awaited him.

At one o'clock in the morning a few weeks later, I sat straight up in bed and looked around my bedroom. I had no idea what woke me up, but an eerie silence engulfed me. I dragged myself out of bed and shuffled down the hall to Brian's bedroom. My heart sank and started pounding in my chest when I saw his empty bed. He was fifteen years old, and I had no idea where he was.

I visualized every possible catastrophe from a car accident to a drug overdose, convinced my son would be returned to me in a body bag. A still, summer night—so often enjoyed for its softness and peace—took on a new meaning. It became a source of terror and anguish as I waited for his return. I sat on the edge of the bed and rubbed the back of my neck. My chest tightened as panic set in. I got up and began pacing in the hallway as my mind swirled with questions, *What can I do? Should I call Ed? The police?*

My great-grandmother Rose Ranze came to me in a memory. I was eight years old. The light blue wall matched the veil in The Blessed Virgin Mary's portrait hanging over her bed. As I peered from the hallway, I saw Grandma Ranze wrapped in a pink knit shawl and enthroned amidst fluffy, white bed pillows. Tiny, wrinkled hands clutched crystal

Rosary beads, and she prayed with such fervor I was afraid to disturb her.

As I entered her room and approached her bed, she opened her eyes and smiled, reaching out to grasp my hand. With Rosary beads dangling, she continued to murmur her prayers, a soft, soothing drone.

"Katadina, sit-a-here," she motioned, making the sign of the cross and kissing the tiny silver crucifix on the Rosary.

I sat on the edge of the bed, and she pulled me close. Her Rosary beads tickled the back of my neck as I melted into her embrace.

"God bless. God bless," she whispered. The musty scent of age lingered as she gently rubbed my neck. Her hands felt smooth, like a soft, leather glove.

Saying the Rosary made me feel close to her.

I returned to my bedroom, grabbed my Rosary beads from the bedpost, and sat in bed, praying each Hail Mary out loud, stopping every once in a while to plead with God to return my son home to me safely. An hour later, I finally heard the sound of the side door opening. I got out of bed and met Brian at the top of the stairs.

"Hi, Mom," he said, like he was coming home from school in the afternoon—not wandering in at 2:00 a.m.

I had no words as I stood there, vacillating between extreme relief, terror at what could have been, sadness, guilt—a wide range of feelings that rendered me speechless. *Was I immobilized with fear? Ashamed that I was not controlling my son? Was I simply relieved he was home?* It would have been a perfect opportunity to involve Ed in a plan to make Brian accountable for sneaking out. I hate to think that I had given up. The guilt I carried about putting both my children through so many moves and subjecting them to an abusive second husband took over and clouded my sense of reason. I felt locked in place.

"Mom, don't worry," he said. "I'm doing okay."

When I turned to look at him, he had already retreated to his room, softly closing the door behind him.

A few days later, when I managed to gather my thoughts, I left my son a card on his dresser. I had written my deep concerns about his leaving the house in the middle of the night.

When he read it, he approached me with tears in his eyes.

"Mom, I had no idea this would affect you this way," he said, brushing his hand across the top of his head. "Don't worry, Mom. Nothing bad is happening."

"Brian, I want to believe you, but sneaking out in the middle of the night can't be good. Where are you? What are you doing? Who are you with?" I said. Words I couldn't find a few nights ago found their way to the surface.

I don't remember what his answers were—did I block them out? But I do remember his wide eyes as he said, "Nothing happened, Mom." The fact that he didn't reassure me gave me constant cause to stay on high alert. The need to take action took on an immediacy I could no longer deny. And yet, I didn't take immediate action. I wonder if, despite all the evidence mounting before me, I was still hoping he'd somehow wake up and pull out of it. My denial was that strong. Or was it fear? As I look back, I believe denial had overcome reason.

The terror of his risky behaviors escalated in the months after we moved to Main Street. As I pulled into the driveway one night, a few indefinable figures exited my front door and disappeared in evening shadows. When I walked inside, empty beer cans cluttered a corner of my dirt-floor basement, reminding me of the empty beer cans surrounding Ed's corner chair. In retrospect, it was all blatant evidence before me that Brian was drinking and having friends over, but I still stumbled along, trying to make sense of his behavior. I never caught him in the act of drinking. In my weaker moments, I still clung to the hope that Brian was in a teenage phase he'd eventually outgrow, like I was waiting for the drinking to magically disappear. But the fear of his behavior never went away.

"We're all scared for him," Simon confessed at Ethan's Eagle Scout ceremony in March of 1991, six months after we moved to Main Street. Brian was noticeably absent, still in bed on that Sunday afternoon. Brian's good friends—Donald, Ethan, Simon, and Jonathan—surrounded me at the ceremony.

"He keeps hanging out with the scumbags."

"We've tried to talk with him."

"He really needs help."

"I saw him drinking in his room one Saturday when you were shopping."

As I stood listening, an intense sadness enveloped me. These fifteen-year-olds were all struggling with their own challenges of peer pressure and raging hormones. Their moms had verbalized concerns to me about them hanging out with the wrong crowd or getting some girl pregnant. But these young men seemed to know the line not to cross, and if they did cross it, they seemed to learn their lessons about friends and risky activities the first time around. Hearing his friends' genuine concern for Brian broke through my denial that this was a normal teenage phase. Brian needed help, and it was up to me to get it for him.

While I was actively trying to develop a plan for helping Brian, emergency late-night meetings and a budget crisis that set off alarms about hospital bankruptcy kept all the hospital employees on edge. For me, it served as a distraction from the brewing crisis at home. Ultimately, the board canceled the management contract and terminated the top-level management team, which included me.

I was pleased that I was able to fall back on my nursing career, and, soon after, I landed a job teaching nursing at a nearby college. During this time, Brian would go through uneventful phases where he did his homework and stayed out of trouble. And, baseball was always a reprieve from drinking and staying out at night.

Around this time that my work and personal life were reaching a crisis point, I had discovered that parents were having parties in their homes and serving alcohol so that their kids would stay home rather than be out drinking and driving. The parents encouraged this by having the kids leave their car keys at the front door.

"What about the kid who leaves the party on foot and collapses in a snowbank or gets hit by a car as he staggers alongside the road? What about my kid?" On the phone, I begged the parents for answers to those questions, but no one seemed to care. I was fighting not only my son but a whole community of parents who not only condoned but sponsored such activities, as if they were trying to be their child's best friend. In exasperation, I phoned the school superintendent. I was advocating not only for Brian but also for myself, a single mother trying her best to overcome the obstacles.

"Sam, I think it is totally inappropriate as well as illegal for parents to be serving alcohol to minors in their homes," I said.

"I'm sorry, but it is not within the jurisdiction of the school system to monitor what people do in their homes," he said in a sterile, rote manner, like he had repeated it many times before to others. "There is nothing I can do about it."

I could feel the blood rush to my head and my breathing quicken, even though his logic made sense. How could I have expected him to have any control about what people did in their own homes? But I wasn't feeling rational. I was scared for my son.

"And that's it—just like that? In other words, it's not your problem that my son has a drinking problem," I said, by now feeling livid and disheartened. My heart was racing, and my thoughts were a blur. I wanted to scream.

"I understand your frustration, but my hands are tied."

"Well, I just hope and pray my son comes out of this alive," I said, slamming the phone down. I had to make sure I had a plan to help my son.

One day, I noticed Brian favoring his right hand as he walked up the stairs.

"What's wrong with your hand, B? Let me take a look."

"Oh, it's nothing, Mom"

His hand was swollen and bruised.

"How did this happen? Were you in a fight?"

Silence.

I later found out from his friends that he was drunk at a house party over the weekend and had fallen down the basement stairs.

When I confronted him, he begged me not to call the parents for fear of getting them in trouble.

I dialed the number of the parents who'd held a drinking party Brian had attended only to hear the same litany of rationale and justification for serving alcohol to minors.

"My son fell down your stairs and injured his hand at your party, and you're telling me it's alright to serve alcohol?" I said. Again, I hung up feeling as helpless, furious, and frustrated as ever.

Granted, I knew it was not other parents' responsibility to monitor and control my son, but there wasn't even an attempt to listen to my concerns. I felt so alone in my quest to help my son. It made me realize the stigma surrounding underage drinking. The silence and lack of support from other parents amplified my sense of fear and loneliness.

Nowadays, parents are prosecuted for such offenses, but back then, my concerns were only discounted, further adding to my sense of isolation as a woman who advocated for her child. I went to school functions burdened with shame about my son's drinking, comparing myself to the parents of other teens. Despite knowing that other parents condoned drinking, I felt like my lack of control over Brian reflected badly on my parenting skills. It was a vicious cycle that left me weary and defeated. I was sinking as fast as Brian.

"Mom, he ruined my bicycle" Leigh Ann screamed. "I hate him."

"Mom, you let him get away with so much."

"Brian, what ever happened to the new outfit I just bought you?" I asked.

"Brian, what happened to the jar of quarters in my bottom dresser drawer?"

"Brian, I found this pipe in your car."

"Brian, did you use my car?"

"Mom, I just got picked up for speeding, and they found an empty beer can in my car," Brian said.

And so it went . . .

"Hello, Coach Frank," I answered the phone one day at work.

"Sorry to bother you at work, but Brian was seen with Anthony Lee during school hours. Anthony is a mental patient who put an axe through his front door one day."

"My God!"

"Yeah, Brian needs to stay away from him. He's trouble."

Coach Frank was the director of the school sports program and had given us an enthusiastic welcome when we moved to the area. I was encouraged that Brian was surrounded by coaches, male role models who cared about his welfare.

I tried talking with the academic teachers to see what could be done.

"I want Brian to participate in the Odyssey of the Mind for Math at the community college, but he doesn't seem interested," Brian's Math teacher said.

"Brian had the highest average in physics in the beginning of the year," Brian's Physics teacher said, "but he just failed his exam."

"I think Brian needs to be sent to Marine boot camp or to some isolated island where he will be forced to learn survival skills. He is impossible to teach," Brian's English teacher reported as she sat straight up in her chair, tilting her head and putting her nose in the air. I bristled at her negative comment, though I totally understood why she felt frustrated about Brian's behavior.

"Brian is a smart student," Brian's Spanish teacher said. "He just needs to stop trying to be the class clown."

"Ninth-grade boys are like a disease," Brian's Social Studies teacher said.

Even his friends chimed in,

"Geez, man. When are you going to start thinking about your future?" one of Brian's friends, Jonathan, asked as I stood by, watching him flick his middle finger on Brian's temple and wishing that would nudge him in the right direction.

In the spring of 1992, I awakened to headlines in the local paper about one of Brian's other friends, Justin, who was busted for drugs. I had heard his name and knew the family from church but had no idea he was involved in drugs. I shuddered at the recognition of several other names, relieved that Brian was not one of them. But I also secretly wished Brian could have been caught so he could get some help. I wasn't sure how to get him this help.

The clues remained as clear and obvious as ever. I walked a tight rope of denial, knowing deep down that Brian needed help but still hoping he'd pull out of this cycle of drinking, waking up, hitting bottom, getting scared, and changing. But it was never like that. Between Ed and Brian, I had spent the past twenty years dealing with the agony of wishing and waiting for someone else to change. I had dealt with walking away from his father when the drinking did not stop. Having a son with a drinking problem was new and different. I could walk away from Ed, but I could not—nor did I want to—walk away from Brian.

It seemed I always had an excuse for Brian's intolerable behavior, linking it to my poor choices of men and feeling guilty about traipsing through Pennsylvania, Wisconsin, and Missouri and back home to New York in search of a better life. I can see how my guilt fed my enabling behaviors.

Soon after Justin was busted for drugs, I ran into Brian in front of the Amana stove as he staggered into the kitchen. I looked into his eyes as he stared into space. I looked at his haggard face and knew he was slipping away right in front of me. It was just a matter of time before he'd slip away forever. I had already grieved the loss of that sensitive, caring little guy who'd once stood up for his friends who were bullied; the one who held so much promise for making a positive difference in the world. Even though I didn't quite have an action plan, I knew I had to find a way, or alcohol would steal him away forever.

"Where are you, Brian, and how can I get you back?" I cried, horrified and helpless as I grabbed his slumped shoulders and shook him.

He looked beyond me with a hollow expression and didn't answer; then he turned away and went to his bedroom as I leaned on the stove and sobbed. I knew in that moment that I was losing my son, and I could wait no longer to take action. I could no longer deny the seriousness of his drinking as I had been doing since the first time I'd seen him drunk, in 1990.

The next day, I called Shelley, the school counselor, to set up some sessions. After several sessions with Shelley and me, it finally became apparent that an intervention with Brian was in order. I scheduled an appointment with Shelley and held my breath until I could get Brian to her office.

CHAPTER 6

The Glow of Denial, 1992

Within a week of scheduling the counseling session, Brian and I met with Shelley, the school counselor.

"Brian, do you understand your mom's concern about your drinking?" Shelley asked, leaning forward in her chair. Her voice was soothing and firm, which immediately signaled a sense of control, something I had lost and needed to reclaim.

"No—she's getting hyper for nothing," he fired back, looking down at his feet as he tapped his heels on the floor repeatedly.

Shelley and I exchanged glances. She was a fashion statement, with her long black skirt and bright turquoise paisley, fringed scarf draped over a soft white blouse. Her dangling silver earrings and thick silver bracelet completed her exquisite look and made me feel like she was in charge—not to mention her calmness. It was a sharp contrast to how scattered I was feeling about how Brian's life was at stake.

I felt so inept in my ability to handle his drinking and the resulting defiant behavior. I waited for her next move as I looked over at her. With a look of genuine compassion that felt like a hug, she leaned in toward him with her hands on her knees.

"Brian, you are a fine young man with lots of potential." She paused and then continued, "We want you to succeed."

I fought back some tears as I nodded in agreement. We all sat suspended in silence for a few moments.

It was early March 1992, and I held myself back from interrupting the meeting dozens of times just like I had held myself back from admitting him to an adolescent substance-abuse rehabilitation program.

After briefly explaining the rehabilitation program, she said,

"Will you agree to attend a program for a few weeks that will help you? You will learn about yourself."

I shifted in my chair, feeling a twinge of guilt for manipulating this rehabilitation decision and packing his bags ahead of time. I breathed in and out in slow, measured breaths, conscious of the stakes.

"Alright. I guess I'll go," he muttered, still looking down.

I exhaled slowly. *Now all I have to do is drive him there.*

"Okay—that's a good decision, Brian. I'll make a phone call." Shelley nodded and stood up to leave, looking back as she opened the door. "Be right back."

I felt an instant relief until I thought about the next step of driving him there. The facility was twenty-five miles away.

Brian and I were alone and sat in mutual discomfort. He glared at me.

"I'm not going, Mom," he said, slinking back in his chair with his arms folded tightly across his chest.

"Let's just see what Shelly finds out," I replied, feigning a calm I didn't feel.

"M-o-o-o-m—why are you doing this to me?" he asked, with a probing gaze and a furrowed brow.

"I love you, B," I said as I leaned in and zeroed in on his eyes. They were soft and vulnerable, reminding me of the little boy I had fallen in love with.

"I just don't want to lose you," I said. Tears threatened to flood me.

For a moment, I felt strong in my words and intentions. For the first time, I felt a sense of empowerment. I allowed myself to be consoled by his silent recognition that he needed help, though I knew he would continue fighting it.

Our silence was broken when Shelley bounded into the room, smiling and energetic.

"Good news. We're all set. Just go to the first-floor admissions office. Here are the directions," she said as she handed me a piece of paper.

"Good luck, Brian. This is an important step you are taking," she said, holding out her hand to shake our hands.

He smiled, nodded in response, and accepted her handshake.

I felt comforted by her compassion. I was walking a tightrope between hope and despair, fighting to stay on the side of hope that Brian would get the help he needed and go on to live up to his potential.

We got in the car without any resistance and continued our silence. As the trees and rolling hills along the highway whizzed past us for the thirty-minute ride down Route 88 to Conifer Park, the rehabilitation facility, we were occupied with our own thoughts.

Finally, we arrived at a large brick building set back among a canopy of tall evergreen trees in a neatly groomed residential section. The sign out front noted it used to be a Tuberculosis (TB) sanatorium. I recalled from my nursing school days that TB sanatoriums were places of healing in bucolic settings. It felt like a haven to me. I said a silent prayer: *Thank you, Lord.*

When Brian opened the passenger door and hopped out of the car, I noticed a bounce in his step. Maybe he was enthusiastic, even relieved? I knew I was.

As I watched him open the door and walk in, I soaked up the consolation and relief. I parked the car and met him in the waiting room, feeling safe for the first time in a very long time.

Our last name was called for the admission process, and we both participated in answering routine demographic questions. Then Brian was called to meet individually with a young male counselor—a tall, thin man with thick black curls. At that point, I wondered what I was supposed to do. Soon after, a petite middle-aged woman with bleached-blond curly hair, who, I later found out, was a counselor, called my name, and I followed her, not quite sure what to expect.

It was interesting and even a little disarming that I was assigned a counselor. I soon found out that I was being introduced to the concept that alcoholism was a family disease and that everyone needed counseling to get better. Even though I had studied family-centered nursing for years, the concept gave me a strange feeling, like I was in a foreign country and could not speak the language. I felt a twinge of defensiveness. *What have I done wrong? I thought I was doing the right thing by bringing my son here.* I didn't realize that I would be considered a patient as well.

This, I learned, was the first step in recovery. It was not as simple as I'd envisioned. I was on the road to recovery, too. There were two other people involved—Leigh Ann and their dad, Ed—but, at that point, it was just me.

For the three weeks that Brian stayed in the program, I visited him only on the weekends. Phone calls were restricted for the first week, so this was the first contact I'd had with him since admission. He looked rested, and his eyes were clear. Overdue for a haircut, he looked a little shaggy, with strands of hair jutting out. But he was alive and getting help, and I felt relieved. During this visit, we walked into the family room, and I noticed framed sayings on each wall with "One Day at a Time." "The Twelve Steps." "One drink is too many, and a thousand are not enough." Addiction treatment was a whole new world, with its own language. I wondered how Brian was reacting to the program. Mostly, I wondered if his stay was making a difference. *Was he open to the help or just putting in his time? Will he do what he is supposed to do to get well?*

During this visit, Matt, his counselor, told me of a fifteen-year-old male patient who died within two weeks of discharge from the program. The thought of no guarantees left me feeling even more unsettled than I was already feeling. Seeing him at the facility confirmed my fears about his drinking leading to addiction and made me wish I had taken action sooner.

"Mom, I'm doing OK," Brian said as we sat in the room, scanning the signs on the wall.

"Show me what you're learning, B."

He handed me his workbook with scribbles and doodles all over, amidst The Twelve Steps and the soul-searching questions that must be answered about who your friends were and what kinds of activities you were involved in: "People, Places, and Things."

"Mom, did you know there are three places I can go if I keep drinking?" he asked.

"No—tell me."

"Jail, institution, or death," he said with a chuckle.

"Well, that doesn't sound very funny to me," I said, feeling disturbed by his glibness.

"Do you really think this is a joke?"

"No, Mom. But I'll be glad to get out of here," he said, looking downward.

"Look at me, B," I said. "I hope you'll use this time to learn about yourself and get some help."

At that, a scruffy-looking, middle-aged male counselor with a graying beard and a pot belly stood in the doorway and bellowed out orders,

"Hey, Brian. I thought you were told to clean your room earlier," he said, his hands on his hips.

"Yeah, but my mom's here," he said, jutting his chin out and smirking.

"You think you are so slick, Brian," the counselor said. "Well, we have rules around here, and you can't manipulate your way around them, so get a move on."

"Visiting hours are over, B. I'm going to leave," I said, after being there for two hours. Bending down to grab my purse, I felt relieved that someone else besides me, especially a strong male role model, was in charge of Brian.

Brian slowly swaggered to his room with a smirk on his face, acting like he'd won that one.

I stood in the doorway, shaking my head as I watched him amble to his room. He turned, nodded, and flashed me a faint smile and a thumbs-up as he stood in his doorway. The thought of him being discharged within the week terrified me. But I still clung to hope that the three weeks would "fix" him.

The day before Brian was discharged, Ed and I attended the family session, in which we sat in a big circle with several other young men and their families. We were told it was the truth-telling session. Truth telling, and breaking the cycle of lies, are considered the cornerstones of addiction recovery.

"Now, Brian, it's your turn to be honest with your parents," Brian's counselor, Matt said, gesturing to Brian. I shuddered when I heard those words and wondered what Brian would reveal.

Shuffling in his chair and clearing his throat, Brian looked over at us and paused before he spoke. This time, he looked humbled and serious.

"Well, I have some things to tell you guys that I'm not proud of," he began, as we looked at him with anticipation and dread. He continued,

"One night, Jeff and I broke into the Country Club and stole some money from the cash register."

I gasped out loud, put my hand up to my mouth, and sat in stunned silence. I looked over at Ed, whose eyes widened in response.

It confirmed what I already suspected—Brian had been lying for the past three years. Ed and I turned to look at one another with a mixture of sadness and resignation as Brian went on in a litany of confessions.

"Mom, I've taken your car while I was drinking, and I've had parties at the house when you were at meetings."

All the inklings of wrongdoing I had suspected came to life before me in flashy, gritty detail.

When it was over, I leaned toward Ed.

"As hard as it was to hear the truth, I do feel some consolation in his honesty."

"Agreed," Ed nodded.

Ed tended to be passive and nonchalant, but this was the first time I ever saw that he and I were really on the same page. There was a ray of hope that we had reached a turning point, in our relationship as parents *and* with Brian.

On the day of his discharge, I wondered how we could all work together now that he had gotten a taste of professional help. We were advised to go home and "work the program." Brian and I were assigned to local counselors and were instructed to attend support-group meetings in our area. I couldn't help but feel fueled with much-needed hope.

On the sunny March day Brian was discharged in 1993, I welcomed him home with a special party at the house, complete with a homemade banner across the living room doorway. My favorite picture of him was taped to a banner, with colorful balloons on the entryway from the dining room into the living room. A photo of him perched on the branch of a large maple tree brilliant with gold and red leaves showed those bright, dancing eyes and told a story of a mischievous, fun-loving ten-year-old. All his good buddies—Don, Simon, Ethan, and Jonathan—gathered around him, giving him bear hugs and taps on the head. I could tell they were relieved that Brian had gone for help by their lighthearted banter and laughter. The table was full of deli platters, chips and dip, and a rectangular bakery cake with "Welcome Home, B" in the center.

Brian, age ten, in Amery, Wisconsin

How can he go wrong with all this goodness around him? Fran had stopped by to help, and we both chuckled as the boys wrestled each other and joked around. These friends loved Brian and were uncomfortable with his drinking and choice of other friends who did drugs. They wanted him to get better as much as I did. The question was: Did *Brian* want to get better?

Initially, once Brian got released from the treatment program, he received a sponsor, a person who had achieved sobriety and would serve as a mentor in recovery. We were expected to attend regular Alcoholic Anonymous and Al-Anon meetings, as well as weekly counseling sessions at a local outpatient counseling center, for as long as necessary. Once again, I was filled with hope as we began our outpatient follow-up program.

At my first Al-Anon meeting in a church hall, just one week after his discharge, I openly shared about Brian's rehabilitation program. For the first time since I had come to terms with Brian's drinking, I finally understood what it meant to sustain hope and felt inspired to take my newfound awareness of addiction and my role in it to create some stability and peace in our family. But I still had a way to go.

"He's doing so well. Life is so good now that he's not drinking," I said, gloating and entertaining the idea that I really didn't even need to be there. Even though I had faced my son's addiction, denial still had a hold on me.

The members, mostly older women and a few young men, gave me blank expressions. *Why aren't they congratulating me in this success?* I wondered.

"Well, that's good, Kathy, that your son went to rehab," Alice, the group leader said, adding "but you need to work the Al-Anon program for yourself." I had yet to know exactly what that meant.

I sat, listening but taking offense to what she was saying—*How dare she burst my bubble of hope?*—as she continued,

"What if he relapses? How will you handle that? Are you prepared?"

I looked around the room in astonishment as the rest of the group looked over at me and nodded "Yes." I did not want to listen to their message. In time, I would grow to appreciate the wisdom of these veterans of alcohol battles. They had learned to survive and grow through the ravages of living with and loving an alcoholic, as I had yet to learn.

But for the time being, I hung on to the glow of denial, choosing to believe that my son had been cured by this three-week stint in rehab.

CHAPTER 7

The Good Sibling, 1991

While I was consumed with Brian's escapades, Leigh Ann stayed in the background of my struggles with him, keeping busy with school, sports, and her friends. She was a hard worker and minimized contact with both of us. That made me feel sad and guilty that I wasn't there for her. She had gotten used to not having me around because I was so obsessed with Brian.

Since we had moved to Cobyville, I looked to Leigh Ann as a source of strength, though I frequently reminded myself that I was the adult and she was the child. Leigh Ann tested the limits, but if she stepped over the line, she learned her lesson. One night she was caught drinking with several of her friends at a local quarry.

"Mom, I have something to tell you that I'm not proud of. Lisa, Laura, and I were hanging out with a few guys at the quarry and got picked up for drinking," she said when she came home that night.

"The worst part is," she continued, "my name will be in the paper." Her hazel eyes were filled with regret as she looked down at her feet.

"Thanks for being honest, honey," I said, putting my hand on her shoulders and looking in her eyes. "I trust you will take this lesson to heart and make better choices."

She quickly made the connection between her activities and her reputation and decided to use that episode as a lesson for herself. I felt relieved. My daughter seemed to have an inner compass. Maybe I wasn't such a bad parent after all.

Leigh Ann learned to choose her activities wisely so she could maintain her status as an honor student and star basketball player.

But our relationship was strained throughout her teen years, which I rationalized was not terribly unusual for a single mother and a teenaged daughter. I thought of my own upbringing and how my father was right there for me. I had a sense of security that he would protect me. It pained me to know what my children were missing by not having their father around to guide and protect them.

We were all tangled up in our own pain, a pain we couldn't openly identify—Brian skirting around us, lying about his whereabouts, Leigh Ann avoiding spending time at home and not engaging in conversation. If any of her friends were from two-parent families, she jumped at the chance to visit their homes, and I was left wringing my hands and losing sleep. She needed emotional stability, and I was anything but stable. I tried the best I could, attending all Leigh

Ann's basketball games and cheering my heart out, only to have her evade me after the game.

"I really like going to Ted's house," she said about her classmate within the first year of our move, scooping her thick brown curls into a ponytail. "I want to experience being a family."

I felt so sad for not being a two-parent family, even jealous of Ted's family. Had I had the tools to manage my own triggers and self-pity, I would have been able to be more emotionally present for Leigh Ann instead of defending myself and Brian's poor decisions.

"He gets away with everything, Mom," she said one day, the words flying out of her mouth like sharp barbs across the room, continuing with a litany of demands.

"Make him pay for the bicycle he ruined," she said and then continued, "Make him apologize for losing my favorite windbreaker, which he probably sold for drugs."

"Leigh Ann, I understand your frustration, but your brother has a drinking problem and needs help," I said, hoping she'd understand.

Every time she spewed these words, I cringed and fell deeper into a pit of helplessness and shame about my role as their mother. Then the guilt about having no control overwhelmed me, clouding any clear-cut means of dealing with it effectively. Mostly, I felt scared to death Brian would end up like his father, never living up to his potential because of the choices he was making, if he ended up living through it.

It never occurred to me at the time that Leigh Ann's caustic remarks were a plea for help. But I was beginning to see the inner turmoil she must be experiencing. She needed stability, but her life was surrounded by the chaos of an addicted brother and a preoccupied mother. She sought refuge in sports, school, and the homes of her friends. She rolled her eyes, shot me cold glares, walked away, or basically steered clear of our home. She rarely confided in me about her deepest concerns. She hardly talked to me at all, which made me feel awkward and inadequate as her mother.

She was the older sister fuming in the background, arms crossed and a scowl on her face, while Brian manipulated his way around me like a slick pickpocket, sneaking out at night, skipping school, stealing clothes, and basically doing whatever he felt like doing. I stood by wringing my hands, losing sleep, feeling incompetent and helpless. I felt like I was on the back of a young stallion on his first run of the spring, holding on for dear life as I pulled the reins in with all my might.

"Mom, Lisa wanted me to go to a party where they'd be smoking pot," she said soon after her name was in the paper for drinking at the quarry. "I told her 'No.'"

I smiled as I looked over at her and felt a burst of pride in my daughter's ability to set healthy boundaries for herself. I knew it was hard earned. Her thick, brown curls framed her face, and she had a look of resolve as she stood erect and fixed her gaze on me. Her display of empowerment gave me hope that we could get through this period of fear and uncertainty. It didn't change that Brian's life was at stake, but it did give me hope that she was developing the life skills needed to cope with challenges.

CHAPTER 8

A Safe Port in the Storm, 1992

At the age of forty-six, twice divorced, with two teenaged children, I figured finding love again was probably not going to happen. My faith in God and the support of a loving family had guided me through many trials. Since escaping two emotionally abusive marriages over a span of twenty-five years, I settled on the thought that my happiness was more important than finding Mr. Right. This revelation was freeing once I realized I didn't need Richard, whom I had dated for a few months until I severed ties, due to the ongoing interferences with his mother and his strained, distant relationship with his two children.

Somewhere, deep inside, I still held out for a man who would be worthy of me.

A few nights after leaving Richard in the café in October of 1992, I reached out to my journal, asking God to send me a stable, caring man. I had to know he was from God and not from my own desperate need to provide my children with an intact family life.

Three days after writing in my journal, Fran and I went back to the singles dance at the Polish Community Center, which I had been attending for more than a year. A few men had stumbled my way whom I dated casually and sporadically. But as soon as I figured out that they weren't compatible, I ended the relationship. To be alone was not the worst fate. I had learned the hard way that being in a relationship that wasn't working was not worth the struggle. To finally claim this understanding after so many years was liberating.

In November of 1992, I convinced two of my co-workers to join me at an evening dance. Fran's boyfriend, Henry, an immigrant from Germany, slipped away from us as I gathered around Fran and my two friends. As the four of us women stood in a semi-circle chatting about the awkwardness of being single again, Henry led a tall, ruggedly handsome man to our circle, leaving us alone again.

"Hi. I'm Wayne," he said, reluctantly.

I sidled up next to him, leaned in, and held out my hand, "Kathy. Nice to meet you."

I had seen him before at a previous dance and had been attracted to him from afar, but I never gave it any more thought.

Now, as I stood next to him, I took notice of his quiet, down-to-earth look, like the Marlboro man from the 1970s commercial, only without the cigarette hanging out of his mouth. Dressed casually in a blue plaid shirt and tan corduroy pants, he immediately struck me as someone I could approach if I were ever in trouble. His eyes were soft blue and kind, and his smile, gentle, with an edge of shyness. I felt my pulse in my throat and wanted him to stay beside me.

We all chatted until Wayne and I began talking to each other. Soon the others faded into the background. Just me and this man.

"Would you like to dance?" Wayne asked.

"Sure."

I was intrigued but reluctant. I had recently vowed to not get involved with another man for a while.

Still, I felt a sense of ease, lightness, and excitement as we floated in harmony out onto the dance floor.

Over the next few months, Wayne continued to pursue me, but I shied away as I recalled the deep hurt I had experienced in previous relationships. In December 1992, he reached out to me a second time, asking if I'd like to go to dinner.

I liked Wayne but was not certain how much to get involved. I hesitated and said, "I guess so," still unsure of the prospect of introducing a new man into our chaotic lives.

After a moment of silence, he said,

"Are you going to go out with me or not?"

His willingness to be honest and his forthright nature relieved me. It convinced me how important it was to allow myself to trust the flush of new love or infatuation. It was too early to tell if it was really love, but I decided to give him and myself a chance to find out. Maybe Wayne was different and would end up being the love of my life. I would have to chance the risk of getting involved again and trust in my ability to know if dating Wayne was right for me. My two previous failed marriages made me skittish about getting into another relationship, yet I knew I wanted to give love another chance—to give myself permission to trust.

"Yes, Wayne," I said. "Absolutely yes!"

CHAPTER 9

Love Conquers All, or Does It? 1992–1994

Over the next two years, Wayne and I saw each other on the weekends, traveling the forty miles back and forth between Burnt Hills and Cobyville while maintaining our out-of-town jobs.

Although I was reluctant to introduce a new man into our lives, I also felt comforted to be able to share my concerns with someone who understood what it was like to be a single parent with a rebellious son. Our sons were both struggling to find their way in the world; that challenged our parenting abilities.

Brian and Sam kept us both on our toes and challenged our sanity and will at every juncture. Sometimes they took turns acting out—drugs, alcohol, reckless driving, wrong crowds. We spent hours commiserating on the phone while our boys were off wreaking havoc in unknown places, leaving us feeling powerless and defeated. When his son Sam wasn't crashing cars into telephone poles and spewing profanities in response to limits set, Brian was sneaking out at night, coming home glassy-eyed and surly.

One night, as I eased into the hot bubble bath I had drawn in my claw-foot tub and let the warm water wash away or at least soften my fears, the phone rang. I was expecting to hear from Wayne, so I kept the phone by the tub.

"Well, Sam did it up big this time." Wayne said, sounding like I felt, weary and worn.

"Now what?"

"I walked in early from my Boston meeting and found Sam and a few of his friends getting ready to party at the house. When I walked through the door, his friends scattered, and Sam went berserk, throwing things and shouting obscenities at me as he tried to body slam me against the wall. I was so frustrated, I called the police to restrain him."

"Oh, my gosh! How scary!" I said. "He really needs help. Did you get hurt?"

As badly as I felt for Wayne, I also felt a shiver of relief that I was not the only one dealing with an out-of-control teenaged son. I began to trust that Wayne could understand the trials of a single parent.

"No, but he's getting too strong for me to handle physically. I had him sent to Four Winds (a psychiatric facility specializing in childhood and adolescent mental illness) for evaluation and treatment. He's there now."

"Well, at least you can take a breath, and, hopefully, he'll get the help he needs," I said.

"One can only hope."

Hope. In our own small yet significant way, we held on to each other for hope. The support we offered each other during these difficult moments nurtured our bond.

Over time, it became clearer that what we shared was special and would get us through any other challenge we had to face as a couple. Learning to trust in him was paying off.

Wayne would challenge my parenting, though, telling me what I already knew but didn't want to face. My inability to follow through on limiting behavior was not helping my son. *What was holding me back?* I kept making excuses for his behavior, all centered on his father's abandonment. I can see now that I was playing a victim role.

"But it's different for a mother," I said during one heated exchange a few weeks after Sam's episode. We were sitting at my kitchen table. Brian had been picked up for speeding, and the cops had found an open can and case of beer in his back seat. It was November 1993. Leigh was a sophomore at college; Brian was a high school senior.

"Kathy, I'm not an expert, and I struggle with Sam's outrageous behavior, but you have to let Brian take the responsibility for his reckless behavior. As soon as Sam graduates from high school, he'll be on his own," Wayne said.

"Easy for you to say," I said. "He's rebelling against his feeling of abandonment by his father."

Over the years, I could see the impact that Ed's absence had on my children, their sad faces when he didn't show up, or their frustration when they phoned him and he was drunk. I would often tell him that the kids needed to see more of him, but his life was ruled by alcohol, and my pleas went unanswered.

I still bristled at Wayne's statement each time, though I knew he was right. I started to pace, back and forth across the linoleum floor, saying over and over, "What am I going to do?" It never occurred to me to be angry and proactive about setting limits and consequences for his behavior. Rather, I was mired in despair, wondering where I had failed as a parent.

Wayne got up and walked over to me, putting his arms around me as I sobbed into his shoulder. I melted into his embrace, grateful to have another adult who understood. Still, I was fighting his logic. I knew I had a way to go in finding a way to deal with Brian and the mountain of emotions accompanying the situation.

Rubbing my back, he said, calm and resolute, "Brian needs to start taking responsibility for his behavior."

I looked up at Wayne, our gaze lingering for a while. "Yes, I know you're right."

As much as I knew he was right, I continued to rear up each time Wayne offered his advice to be firmer with Brian. That fierce mother's instinct kicked in when someone else tried to set limits with my child—limits that Brian needed but ones I was not able to follow through on for reasons I didn't understand at the time but later regretted. It would take years and many Al-Anon meetings and prayers for me to break my addiction to his addiction and be able to set firm boundaries for myself and him.

Most of these encounters usually ended with me crying and Wayne standing by patiently, his warm, blue eyes taking in my sorrow.

Both our jobs took us out of town, which set the stage for all kinds of shenanigans such as house parties where alcohol and drugs prevailed. And our neighbors didn't help. Wayne's neighbor didn't want to get Sam in trouble and chose to stay quiet. My neighbors were an elderly couple who lived in a sprawling Victorian home and were hard of hearing.

There were times when the very thing that drew us together—being a single parent of a recalcitrant son—seemed to test the limits of our newfound love. It both tested and strengthened our bond.

But how do you unlock yourself from the story you keep telling yourself? How do you change the script when embroiled in the moment in a desperate struggle to make sense of the harsh reality that your son is spiraling downward and you have no control over it? That the choices you'd made had impacted the lives of your children in ways you never could have imagined? Even when a woman leaves her marriage for all the right reasons, there is still a price to pay.

My overall sense of panic and helplessness usually led me back to Al-Anon meetings. Attending those meetings helped me to break through the denial. It was there I found a safe place to unload my worst fears and crippling guilt. The structure and cadence of the weekly meetings gave me comfort.

Two years later, after Brian moved out of my home, Wayne would often suggest attending a meeting after learning of Brian's latest stints at emergency rooms due to unruly behavior. It was through Al-Anon that I fully comprehended that my son had a disease that I did not cause and could not control or cure. I slowly began realizing that my giving in to his behaviors—paying his bills, making excuses for him—was like handing a suicidal person a gun.

I remembered the passage in the book *Courage to Change*, from November 16, page 32: "Let go and let God." This passage guided the reader to a form of creative visualization, which helped me to get in touch with my spiritual empowerment. I had lost that connection to my Higher Power when the stress of witnessing his drinking overwhelmed me; I needed it more than ever if I wanted to save myself and my troubled relationship with Brian. I envisioned wrapping Brian up in a warm, woolen blanket and gently handing him over to his Higher Power for safekeeping. I had to relinquish the tight control—the worry—over Brian I had created to help him stay alive. In fact, I see now that the control I thought I had over Brian served only to keep the disease alive. I had specific fears, and, at the time, I needed a tangible way of envisioning a solution to my relentless pain and worry. *Control is an illusion. What am I trying to control—Brian's behavior, my response, my living situation? How would it make a difference?* Life happens, and there is so much we cannot alter.

I knew I had found a good man in Wayne, and even though his cool logic would stir a defensive chord in me, I knew he was right. I knew I had to find a way to take back my life. I also knew that I did not want to jeopardize what I knew in my heart was the chance for a healthy, long-term love.

Wayne's presence in my life helped anchor me to reality, and I gradually learned to let go of my need to jump in and save Brian from his self-inflicted wounds. Whenever I felt that weakness come over me to give in to Brian's demands for money, Wayne reminded me how the best way to help Brian was to take care of myself and let him figure out his own way. He assured me,

"Brian is very capable and resilient when left to his own devices."

I needed to lean into Wayne's words and trust that Brian would "find his way home."

Wayne and I endured the next few rocky years, juggling our teenaged sons' extracurricular activities. When our sons moved out after graduating from their high schools in 1994, the challenges mounted.

CHAPTER 10

After his 1994 high school graduation, Brian had been accepted into a post-high school prep school where he also had the opportunity to play baseball. Milford Academy in Milford, Connecticut, claimed to help students transition to a college setting while also playing baseball. I was hopeful this time away would give him a year to mature while enabling him to do something he not only enjoyed but excelled in.

I'd always had this underlying feeling that Brian could do whatever he set his mind to do, as long as he'd quit drinking. However, I had yet to fully comprehend that there was little I could do to change his path, despite acknowledging that I had to let go of this need to influence his behavior in Al-Anon meetings. I poured my hopes and money into the prep school and was encouraged by Brian's enthusiastic response to the opportunity to play baseball year-round.

Initially, he excelled at the prep school and gave me every reason to think this was the answer. But after a few months, the phone calls from the headmaster became increasingly more pessimistic as Brian's drinking continued. My hope fell with each call. His baseball coach was in recovery from alcoholism and tried to help Brian, but Brian had not reached the point of wanting help. After four months, the school agreed to let him finish the semester if he attended a month-long rehab program in Bridgeport, a nearby city. Brian complied with the program and seemed willing to work at his recovery. It was at Bridgeport, his second rehab, that I heard him say with conviction that he was an alcoholic.

"Mom, I know I'm an alcoholic," he said, looking into my eyes as he sat across from me in the family room during a visit. "It's getting easier to say." His eyes were clear and his voice resolute.

"I'm glad to hear you say this, B," I said, reaching over to squeeze his hand.

I looked up at a framed saying on the wall: "One Day at a Time." *Yes, how true, and today is a good day,* I thought.

He successfully completed the twenty-eight-day rehabilitation program and finished the semester with the plan to attend a local college and play baseball. I held my breath as I drove him back home again at the end of the semester, worried that being back home would trigger his drinking again. That summer, he worked on a farm baling hay. Since I was working at a private college as a nursing-faculty member, he was able to attend tuition-free through an exchange program, and we began the preparation for college at St. Rose in Albany, New York.

Again, I had great hopes that this would kick-start him and get him on the right track. I felt reassured that, after a year of prep school and a successful stint in his second rehab, I was cautiously optimistic that he would succeed in college, especially if he was playing on the baseball team.

One Saturday morning two weeks into the fall semester, I received a phone call.

"Mom," Brian said, choking back tears, "I'm in a detox unit."

My heart pounded in my chest as I tried to catch my breath. I wanted to scream, but I knew I had to maintain my control for Brian's sake.

"What happened?" I asked, closing my tear-filled eyes and leaning my forehead into my other hand.

"I started climbing the walls on campus, and security brought me here," he said, like he wondered what the big deal was.

"Mom, I just don't fit in."

I knew how surly Brian became when he drank—spewing his anger and punching walls—though I never knew the true extent of his use. Brian wasn't going to tell me, nor were any of his friends. He scared people with his profanities and tendency toward rage. At six feet one inch, his muscled arms and flushed face, combined with his lack of boundaries, were intimidating.

I visited Brian in the inpatient detox unit before going to work that afternoon in September of 1995. The hospital was next to the medical center where I worked. Brian and I had a phone conference with his counselor, who suggested Brian take the year off to focus on his recovery. This included a second admission to Conifer Park's Alcohol Rehabilitation Program, the same rehab he had attended in high school in 1992. This third chance for Brian to learn from his mistakes and achieve recovery gave me a momentary sense of relief. At least I knew he'd be safe when he was there. I also knew that Ed needed to be notified. I would call him later. Wayne had offered his own perspective on Ed, often reminding me, "Ed loves his kids more than you realize." I don't know how he knew this other than relating to him as father-to-father. This rang in my ears as I pondered updating him while Brian talked to the counselor. Wayne had helped me to see that, although Ed and I didn't see eye-to-eye on the situation, Ed still needed to be included in the conversation. I was beginning to get beyond my own defenses about how to handle Brian and consider the possibility that Ed did love the kids and wanted what was best for them, even though he did not play an active, daily role in their lives.

That same evening, when I went back to the pediatric unit at the medical center, I received another phone call—this time from Coach Bellini, his college baseball coach.

"I'm sorry to say, your son needs help," coach said. "Brian is a great young man with a lot of potential, and I hope he gets the help he needs. He's been acting bizarre, claiming he's "T-1000" and his teammates are concerned about his excessive drinking. We're just not able to keep him on the team." Once again, I wondered where he got the money to buy the booze.

Coach Bellini was enthusiastic about bringing Brian onto the team when we'd gone for the college interview back in June 1995. He had an excellent reputation as one of the best college-baseball coaches in the area, and, at first, I felt excited and hopeful for Brian that he had a positive male role model to guide him.

While his compassion warmed my heart, his ultimatum didn't surprise me. Brian's disease was escalating, and I was helpless to stop it. It felt like another person had taken over my son's body. My sweet, loving son was nowhere to be found. I didn't even like who he had become.

I paused for a moment after hanging up the phone and before going back to work.

Brian's first stint in the detox unit would turn out to be one of many episodes in which I would have to let him find his own way through his setbacks. All I could do was pray and attend Al-Anon meetings. I felt limp with helplessness. I had to learn to surrender and admit I had no control over his behavior, only over my own responses to him. It seemed to me that this tightrope of letting go and surrendering could be tempered only by hanging on to hope.

After a twenty-eight-day stay at Conifer Park, Brian was discharged to a halfway house on Central Avenue in Albany, where he stayed for one year while attending outpatient counseling at Al-Care, a facility within walking distance of the halfway house. He was able to maintain his sobriety—a condition for being able to stay—with this structure and professional help. But I didn't trust his sobriety would last once he was discharged.

I knew I couldn't control Brian, but at least I was beginning to get my own life back. The worry was constant, though, and I continued in weekly counseling sessions. I learned that I held my anxiety in my abdomen, often feeling my stomach knot up in the moments of panic over Brian's activities and future.

"Focus on your physical reactions to the stress," the counselor said, leaning toward me as we sat facing one another. "Tuning into what you are feeling in the moment will help you to eventually minimize the symptom and take back your life."

I closed my eyes and focused on that twisting feeling in the pit of my stomach as my concerns collided with one another—being kicked out of college, wandering around aimlessly at twenty-one, bouncing from one rehab to another with no clear indication that he had any serious intention to stop drinking. *What kind of future was in store for my son? When will he awaken to the realization that drinking is killing him and his chances for a decent life? Will he survive? Will I survive?*

The knot in my stomach did not go away.

Hope was all I had to hang on to as I did the best I could to take care of myself. At least I was learning to put more focus on myself by attending Al-Anon meetings, sharing my feelings, and learning more about myself and my responses to Brian.

CHAPTER 11

Intervention, 1995

I was able to visit Brian at the halfway house. From the outside, the house was worn and weathered, with peeling paint and damaged window shutters. When I first drove into the driveway, I felt like I was driving up to an ill-reputed drug house. But I tried to look beyond the outward appearance and hope that he would get the structure and care he needed to stay sober.

Three months into his stay at the halfway house, Wayne and I participated in a routine, monthly family-counseling session through Al-Care. Wayne and Brian had a tenuous relationship from the start when we first met. They both kept their distance from one another—Wayne not buying into Brian's actions, quietly taking it all in, and Brian steering clear of any confrontation with Wayne.

Jean's office was the size of a large closet, but the family pictures and lush plants surrounding us made me feel welcome. Jean smiled at Wayne, and I felt a gush of appreciation that he was with me.

"We have a lot of concerns about Brian's commitment to the program," Jean said. "He's missed several sessions, and, when he's here, he acts preoccupied. We can't get through to him."

My heart sank. "Will he get kicked out of the program because of non-compliance?"

Jean said, "Not immediately, but we are having a hard time getting a handle on his motivation. There's even a consideration that he acts like a sexual-abuse victim."

Stunned at her words, I sat up straight and tried to make sense of them. "I remember our time in Wisconsin, when I was married to Dan. Brian had been the perfect student until fifth grade, the year we moved there in 1985. During that year, I began getting calls from the teacher that he was disruptive in class."

I wondered if it may have happened then. I would have to ask Brian after the meeting.

Wayne said, "Brian is extremely manipulative and knows what he's doing. I think you should call his father up right now and get him in the loop. Ed loves his kids and is trying to do the best he can."

Again, I bristled at the suggestion, but my growing trust in Wayne's judgment gave me pause to be open to Ed's input.

We reached Ed in two rings, and Jean put him on speaker phone. After introducing herself, she asked,

"Ed, what is your take on Brian?"

Ed said, "I think he needs a one-way bus ticket to Utah so he can figure out what he's going to do with his life."

Jean ended the call.

Wayne nodded and said, “Not a bad idea.”

I shook my head and crossed my arms tight around my chest. “Sure, that’s easy for you to say. You’re not his mother. We don’t even know anyone in Utah.”

It reminded me of the Native American tradition of sending their young men into the wilderness on a vision quest. *How did those mothers handle such a drastic measure?*

Three weeks after this session, we held a family intervention session. My mother traveled from Corning, Leigh Ann came home from college, and we planned to have a phone conference with my three siblings in Corning—Tom, Gary, and Paula—and with Ed, who lived in Syracuse. Mom had little understanding or experience with addiction. I knew it would be hard for her, but it was important that she be a part of this.

Wayne and I picked Brian up at the halfway house and drove him to the session. I had called him that morning at the suggestion of the counselor to let him know about it. If we gave him too much lead time, we feared he would back off. Surprisingly, he agreed without any resistance.

When we entered the large conference room, Mom, Leigh Ann, and Jean were already seated in a circle with a microphone and phone in the middle. Brian took a seat, looking like he was going to have all his teeth pulled without anesthesia. He stretched out in a chair, arms folded, and looked down at his feet before the session started.

Jean called my siblings, who had all gathered at my sister Paula’s house, and Ed, and then opened up the session.

"Brian, today you are going to hear—from the people who love you—exactly how your drinking affects them. You need to understand that it is because they love you and want you to get better that they are willing to share their concerns with you today."

Brian didn't budge from his non-communicative stance, not looking up or acknowledging Jean.

With that, Jean went around the room to give each person a chance to share their thoughts.

"I'm scared you're going to die, B," Leigh said through her tears. "And I hate what your drinking has done to our family . . ."

I looked over at my daughter, and tears welled up in my eyes. I felt her deep pain.

Mom was next, and more tears came.

"Brian, you are such a capable young man, and it breaks my heart to see you wasting your life drinking. Grandpa and I want to see you get better. And we want to see your mother, our daughter, have some peace of mind."

When Tom and Gary spoke on the phone, they both encouraged him to start taking responsibility for his life and reiterated what Mom had said about his capabilities and potential.

But when my sister Paula got on the line, she was sobbing so hard, she couldn't finish her sentence,

"Oh, Brian, please stop . . ."

Brian continued to look down at his outstretched legs. He gave no indication that he'd heard any of what was being said. I put my head in my hands and sobbed as I heard Mom and Leigh's sniffles in the background.

Ed was next, and though I don't remember his exact words, I do remember him repeating his advice about the one-way ticket to Utah.

Wayne sat quietly, taking it all in. When it was his turn, he said,

"It's up to you, Brian, what you do with your life. I hope you make the right decision."

Then it was my turn. I took a deep breath and willed myself to speak my truth.

"The first thing I want to do is ask both my children for forgiveness." I held back the tears while looking first at Leigh and then at Brian.

Leigh looked puzzled and asked, "Why, Mom?"

Brian sat up and looked at me for the first time in the entire session, "No, Mom—for what?"

I said, "For moving you around the country and for not providing you with a stable home. I feel badly about that." I paused to take a breath. "I've been needing to say that. Now that I have, let me say, Brian, you need to stop drinking. Drinking will kill you, one way or another. I don't want to lose you. I agree with what everyone else has said about how capable you are. I am begging you to wake up and get your life back." After a momentary silence, I said, "I love you, and I don't want to lose you."

I continued,

"And Leigh, I feel like you've been lost in the shuffle. I'm so sorry."

"It's OK, Mom," they both chimed in, almost in unison. "It's not your fault."

Not my fault? Did I really just hear my children forgive me?

In November 1996, a few months after I moved in with Wayne, Brian left the halfway house and moved back with us in Burnt Hills under the condition that he attend AA meetings and maintain his sobriety. He got a job through a temp agency twenty-five miles away and agreed to attend AA meetings for a while, but that wore off.

A few weeks after starting his job, he began sneaking out and lying about his whereabouts. Within one month of his return, when we found him drunk in our family room after warning him that not drinking was a condition of his being able to stay with us, we told him he had to leave. It filled me with dread that he was sinking deeper into his addiction and that I was powerless to stop it.

Brian said, "But where will I go?"

It made me furious that he'd put me in this position and deeply saddened that it had come to this. "We'll drive you to a hotel near your job tomorrow."

The next day, I packed a few sandwiches for him, and Wayne and I drove to Central Avenue in Albany, twenty-three miles away, dropping him off at a motel across the street from his new job.

During the short time he lived with us, Brian decided to meet with an Air Force recruiter and began preparing for admission. I was encouraged that he was starting to think about his future and had taken this initiative. I could only hope that he would be able to maintain sobriety long enough to qualify. But after finding him drunk in our family room one night, he went back to the halfway house temporarily and then made arrangements to move to Stamford, a small village in the Catskill Mountains, where he rented a room.

I spoke with him briefly on Thanksgiving Day, 1996.

"Hey, Mom. How's it going?"

"We miss you, B."

The thought of him spending the holiday all alone and missing out on our traditional turkey dinner tore my heart out. But I knew the choices he was making had led to this, and I had to let it go.

He stayed in touch by phone over the next month, and we made arrangements to pick him up on our way to Corning to visit my family over the Christmas holidays. The plan was that he would stay two weeks in Corning and then go live briefly with his sister in her apartment in Albany, where he could prepare for entry into the Air Force in November 1997.

Standing back and letting Brian find his own way left me limp with helplessness. I continued to pray and attend Al-Anon meetings. But in December 1996, some unforeseen health issues would force my hand. I would never give up hope that Brian would recover, but I had yet to learn how hard-earned that would be.

CHAPTER 12

Unexpected Visitor, 1996

In December 1996, six months after turning fifty, my life came to a screeching halt with a cancer diagnosis. I had been living with Wayne for about a month.

On December 19, as I read in bed, I felt a rubbery lump above my left collar bone. That morning, I'd felt a stretching sensation in the area, which I quickly dismissed, along with the persistent, dry cough that had nagged me over the past several months. Even the shortness of breath I had recently experienced when I bent down to clean the cat's litter box did not jolt me into action.

I knew that night the lump meant something serious. I got out of bed and went to the bathroom for a closer look. As I put my hand over my collar bone and rubbed the area, I felt and saw the nodes protruding above it. I also noticed my sunken eyes as I stared listlessly at my image in the mirror. Undeniably—bold and certain—the nodes signaled danger. To be sure, I grabbed my DeGowin and DeGowin book on clinical signs, which reinforced my worst fears. Left subclavicular nodes were *sentinel nodes*—an indicator of an abdominal malignancy.

At eleven at night, the house was silent. I didn't want to awaken Wayne with the news of my findings, but my inability to breathe was alarming. The enormity of that moment as I moved from room to room threatened to overwhelm me. A dog barked in the distance. I felt terrified in my loneliness and tried to still my breathing as I sat on the family room couch and traced the slivers of moonlight on the carpet.

After a few moments, I stood up and walked into the guest bedroom. When I climbed into bed, I noticed that I couldn't lay flat because my breathing became more labored. I began reading about Colonel Custer and the Battle of Little Big Horn. Stories of Custer always kept me spellbound but not on that night. I kept reading the same sentence over and over and realized I couldn't read and breathe at the same time.

I knew I had to wake Wayne. I got out of bed and slowly walked into the bedroom, where I stood by the bed and took in his slow, rhythmic breaths as I tried to get perspective. Breathing continued to be a conscious effort, like I was sucking air from a thin straw. My heart was racing. By then it was hard to know if my breathing was truly worsening or if my anxiety about not being able to breathe freely was taking over. After a few minutes, I could wait no longer. I gently shook his shoulder, and he woke up with a start.

"What?" he said, blinking, his eyes wide open.

"Wayne, I need you to drive me to the hospital."

Before becoming fully awake, he shot out of bed, stumbling in the dark, reaching for his clothes.

"What's wrong?" he asked, pulling up his pants as he reached for the bedside light.

"I can't breathe," I said, taking short, panty breaths and feeling more anxious with each passing moment.

I threw on some sweats and grabbed my beige Timberline boots in the closet. As I bent down to tie the shoelaces, my shortness of breath increased. I had to stop and rest. Wayne bent down and tied them for me.

The cold, crisp December night greeted us as we opened the front door. Wayne held my arm firmly as we walked slowly to the car, my breathing more labored with each step. We drove the fifteen minutes to the hospital, with the moon full and bright, without talking. I struggled to breathe while sitting quietly in the passenger seat. Wayne reached over to hold my hand as we drove along the abandoned road to the hospital in the middle of that clear December night. The bright Christmas lights on the houses we passed reminded me that life goes on despite what's happening in my world—a world that I knew was about to change drastically.

CHAPTER 13

Thief in the Night, December 1996

Wayne stopped the car at the St. Clare's emergency entrance and got a wheelchair. Security escorted me in while he parked the car. *How many times had I wheeled a patient with shortness of breath into a room?* It was hard to relinquish control of caring for others and now be the patient, especially now that I'd graduated from my nurse-practitioner program.

Then the first round of questions: *Are you a smoker? Do you have asthma? When did this start? What brings you here tonight?*

How I had wished this was an asthma-related case and not this dreaded, unknown diagnosis. I had not felt right for months, feeling fatigued, coping with a dry, persistent cough. Over the past few months, the insane summer schedule of traveling to school and clinical sites and working as a part-time pediatric nurse distracted me from the ominous symptoms. *Allergies*, I thought at the time. As I look back on it, I see that nurses really can be the worst patients. We're so busy caring for others that we ignore our own symptoms or at least self-diagnose toward a lesser evil. But the shortness of breath meant I couldn't deny it any longer. When the nurse wheeled me to a stretcher and administered a breathing treatment, my worst fears became real. A nebulizer treatment provided no relief. It was not asthma, and the cause of my symptoms would still need to be identified.

After a chest x-ray, a young doctor with sandy-colored hair and horn-rimmed glasses came to my bedside, holding the x-ray in his hand. A sense of dread washed over me as I prepared myself for his findings.

"I have good news and bad news," he said gently. "Which do you want to hear first?"

"Give me the good news first."

"You don't have a lung tumor," he said, hesitating.

"Go ahead." I felt a momentary relief.

"Your lungs are filled with fluid, which explains your shortness of breath," he said, keeping his calm demeanor.

I pointed to my left subclavicular nodes. They were enlarged, a sign of an underlying systemic problem. "I know what this means." With each passing minute, I anticipated the worst.

He nodded and told me he had arranged for a CT scan of my chest and abdomen to identify the cause of the fluid in my lungs and the enlarged nodes.

After the scan, I was wheeled to a cubicle across the room and hoisted onto another stretcher. It was just myself and another patient in the same room. We were separated by curtains. Wayne was by my side, rubbing my arm, a pained look shadowing his face. We remained speechless. Two hours later, he had to leave to go to work. My breathing had calmed down as I waited for the CT scan results. He leaned down to kiss me; he told me he loved me and would return in a few hours. As soon as he left, I heard the conversation between the other patient and his mother as he droned on in loud tones about having to change his diet, often repeating the same litany: "Cut down on bread, no sweets, no soda." I never did hear his mother talk.

The incessant chatter from across the room grated at me and left me feeling irritated and restless. I sat up on the side of the stretcher and slipped off the side, where I began walking back and forth, still conscious of my labored breathing.

Tears were locked inside. *Not yet*, I thought. *I don't even know what's wrong with me.* I had recently treated a young man with sarcoidosis of the lungs. *Maybe this is not cancer. Maybe what I have is curable*, I tried to assure myself as I continued pacing back and forth.

"Dear Lord," I prayed, "give me the strength, for this is a battle of my life and for my life."

I stared down at my boots, all worn and broken in from hikes in the woods with Wayne. These boots had taken me many miles on hikes through rugged terrain. I knew the terrain was about to get even more rugged, but I also knew I was in unknown territory, lost in the wilderness.

A momentary sense of peace washed over me as I continued my silent, desperate prayer.

When the nurse came by to take my blood pressure, I asked her to help me to the bathroom. As she wheeled me down the empty hall in a wheelchair, I turned to see three doctors leaning into the x-ray viewer box at the nurses' station. They were speaking in hushed tones, nodding to one another while looking at CT films. From what I could tell by their intense concentration and pointing, there were findings to discuss. And since I was the only one in the emergency room who had returned from a scan, I figured it was my film.

When I returned to my stretcher, I looked up at the clock. Four-fifteen in the morning. Pretty soon, I would need to call in to work.

At 7:00 a.m., eight hours after I was admitted, the day-shift ER doctor came to my room with the CT films in hand before Wayne returned.

"You have bilateral pleural (lung) effusions (fluid) and a large mass in your abdomen," he said, shifting his eyes from my chart to somewhere beyond me. He continued, "Which is most likely caused from a type of lymphoma, cancer of the lymph system."

Hearing my greatest fears articulated with clarity and certainty struck a blow. I gasped. Even though I was a nurse, I knew very little about lymphoma. I would soon find out there were hundreds of kinds and various stages.

"Your next step is to have a thoracentesis (lung tap) to identify the cause of the fluid in your lungs," he said,

"Dr. Patel, the pulmonologist, will be in shortly to do this."

I felt like I was standing in quicksand, unable to keep myself from slipping farther down into a pit. *What about my children, Wayne, my family, my job? I want to dance at my daughter's wedding. I want see Brian get sober and stay sober. I want to enjoy my life with Wayne. How can this be? I am the one who usually comforts others. Now what?*

When Dr. Patel arrived a few minutes later, I was relieved by his compassionate manner and soothing voice. He was a slightly built, gentle, young eastern Indian man with big, dark eyes and a pleasant smile that made me want to trust him.

"Hello," he said, reaching out his hands to me.

"I know this must be a very scary time for you, but we will get through this together," he said, as he leaned in and held both my hands with his hands.

"Yes," I said, nodding. "Life as I knew it has stopped." Tears welled in my eyes, but still, I wasn't ready to let loose. I feared I would totally lose control if I started to cry. I had to stay strong for myself. I remembered to breathe.

His eyebrows pulled down in concentration, empathy oozing from every pore.

"I know what you mean," he said. "My wife and I lost our baby girl when she was four months old. Sudden Infant Death Syndrome."

Suddenly, I was compelled to console him. His willingness to share something so sacred and personal strengthened my trust in his ability as a doctor. In that moment, I hoped that I had shown such empathy and concern for my patients when they needed it the most. I needed every ounce of support I could get as I grappled with the reality of my new diagnosis.

After explaining the procedure and having me sign a consent form, he placed a large needle, known as a "trocar," into my back chest wall and drained four quarts of clear beige fluid from my lungs. I gasped from the initial sharp entry of the trocar but slowly began to feel relief as the fluid gushed out into a large bottle.

"I will have the results on Monday," he said, handing me his card and instructing me to call his office to make an appointment for Tuesday.

I looked up at the clock again. By this time, it was seven-fifteen, and I made the call to let the office know I would not be coming to work on that day or any time soon. Wayne walked in as I was talking to my boss.

"We won't know the exact diagnosis until Tuesday," I said.

"Christmas Eve?" he said.

"Yeah. Merry Christmas, sweetie," I said. "This will be one for the record books."

Like a thief in the night, darkness hovered over the Christmas of 1996. I felt robbed of my life as I knew it and wanted it to be.

CHAPTER 14

Christmas Eve, 1996

The evening I returned home from the emergency department on December 19, I called Leigh Ann in her Albany apartment she shared with a high school friend while attending graduate school. Since Brian was staying with her over the holidays, we had made plans to all drive to Corning to see my family. After leaving the halfway house, Brian had decided to enlist in the Air Force. He needed a place to stay until he left for San Antonio in November of 1997.

How will I tell my children I have cancer? My heart pounded as I dialed her number. Leigh Ann picked up on the second ring,

"Hi, honey. I have something to tell you and your brother." The quaver in my voice echoed in my ears.

"Are you OK, Mom?" she said, tentatively. I took a deep breath and decided not to belabor it.

"The doctors think I have cancer, Non-Hodgkin's Lymphoma, but I want you to know that I have a lot of hope that I can beat it. I'll find out for sure on Tuesday."

Silence.

"Leigh, are you OK?"

'Yes, Mom. I know that if anyone can beat it, it will be you."

"Is Brian with you now?"

"No, he went to the store, but he should be right back."

"Please tell him, and have him call me back if he wants to talk about it. Plan on coming over tomorrow so we can talk about it more."

"OK, Mom. We'll see you tomorrow. I love you."

"Love you, too. Be brave. I know God will see us through this."

I knew I had to be brave for my children, but, in that moment, I felt weak as a kitten.

I hung up the phone and sat on the couch, absorbing the reality that life as I knew it was over and that a new chapter stood before me, one that left me with more questions than answers. I shuddered when I thought about my children and vowed to fight with all I had to survive. I had to be there for my children, but I felt shaky and uncertain. So, I did what I had to do. I walked down the hall to the home office, sat at the desk, and began calling my family and friends, one after the other, in all parts of the country.

"The doctors think I have cancer, and I need your prayers."

After three non-stop hours of sharing and tears, I fell on my bed in an exhausted heap, consoled by the love and prayers that enveloped me.

Leigh and Brian came the next day, and I felt even stronger and more determined than ever to fight this disease, whatever it turned out to be, and win. I had so much to live for—my children, my family, my friends who showered me with their love and support. That night, a few days before Christmas, against a backdrop of a shining evergreen tree, Wayne snapped a picture of me surrounded by Leigh and Brian.

On Monday, December 23, 1996, I decided to attend my usual group session for parents with addicted children, even though I was short of breath. I needed to be there. I now needed all the support to face my own health battle, along with the battle with my son. When my turn came to speak, I shared my status with the group and asked for guidance. For many years I had struggled with Brian's drinking, and now I needed to feel safe in asking for support for myself.

"I'm being tested for lymphoma, and I will find out the results tomorrow," I said to the stunned group of three women and two men who looked at me with compassion in their eyes. I was relieved to know they were holding the space for me. I wasn't a separate entity.

"I can refer you to an excellent oncologist, Dr. Valentine," Marsha, one of the other mothers, said. "I was diagnosed with Non-Hodgkin's Lymphoma and have been cancer-free for ten years."

"Really?" I noticed her ruddy complexion and vibrant personality. My sense of hope soared. *Even if it is cancer, I can survive. And thrive. Both the diagnosis and the challenges with Brian.*

On December 24, 1996, five days after going to the emergency room, I prepared for my follow-up appointment with Dr. Patel to find out the result of my thoracentesis. Initially, the shortness of breath had been alleviated by the removal of the fluid, but I was starting to feel the tightness in my chest and a dry cough, which signaled another fluid buildup. When the phone rang, I was not prepared for what I was about to hear.

"Kathy, this is St. Clare's mammography department. We need you to come right down today for an ultrasound. You have a suspicious lesion in your left breast."

What? Isn't it enough that I will find out today the cause of my lung fluid? And then there's Brian and the ongoing terror of his escapades. Isn't this just a little bit ridiculous? Dear Lord, where are you?

"I have an appointment with Dr. Patel at 1:00 p.m. So, I'll be right down this morning," I said, taking a deep breath.

As the technician did my ultrasound, I shared my story with her.

"Oh, I'm so sorry to hear this," she said. "I'll make sure the radiologist reads this right away and comes in to speak with you before you leave."

I was grateful for her kindness. As I lay on the table, waiting to talk with the radiologist, I thought about my friend Judy, who'd lost her battle with breast cancer in

1993. If this was how it was all going to end, I wasn't ready to go or accept that my whole body might be riddled with two terminal diseases. I remembered Judy's strong will to live and her desperate fight against cancer. Losing her was devastating. *Was I going down the same path?*

Thankfully, the radiologist reassured me that the finding looked like a benign cyst. I breathed a sigh of relief, though I still had to face the results of my lung tap. The next stop immediately following the mammogram was Dr. Patel.

As Wayne and I walked into Dr. Patel's office, he greeted us in the same warm way he'd greeted me in the emergency room, with a smile and a handshake. After examining me, he pointed to the two chairs in front of his desk and sat across from us, leafing through some papers. His voice was soft, nearly indiscernible, as I leaned forward to hear his findings.

"You have Non-Hodgkin's Lymphoma and need to be referred to an oncologist," he said, without making eye contact. I could tell he did not want to tell me the news. We were hoping for sarcoidosis, a less-serious condition.

Wayne and I looked at one another as Wayne reached over to squeeze my hand. We weren't married, yet I felt I had a loving, lifelong partner to help me face this challenge.

"I have the name of an oncologist. Dr. Valentine," I said, grateful for Marsha's recommendation. The image of her healthy presence reminded me to stay hopeful.

The weekend after Christmas, Wayne drove me to Corning, and Leigh and Brian drove to Corning in her car. Craving to see my family, my lungs started filling up again, and my shortness of breath worsened. The worries and concerns that I thought I'd managed to let go of for the time being had returned. I had to make arrangements from Corning for another thoracentesis as soon as I returned home on Monday. This was going to be a long and tough battle.

If only there were a treatment plan for my son and his drinking. A week after we returned from Corning, I stood at the kitchen sink in our home in Burnt Hills and looked out at the snow-clad pine trees that surrounded our backyard. In my mother's heart, the cancer diagnosis that had invaded my life paled in comparison to the horror and heartache of watching my son slip down further into his addiction. Thankfully, there were treatment options for the cancer, but there were no options for dealing with my son other than to pray Brian would achieve sobriety and hope I could let go. Right then and there, I made a conscious decision to commit to handing my worries over to God and trust that God would watch over us.

Mary, the leader of my group counseling sessions, had recommended an early-morning program about faith and hope. I tuned in one morning at 5:30 for a program led by a Franciscan priest, Father Peter, and a Dominican nun, Sister Mary Ann of The Bethany Healing Ministry. Their testimony of trusting in God's love and mercy despite all odds touched me at a very deep level and fed the hope that would end up sustaining me in the months to come.

Following treatments a few months later, I attended a local retreat at the Dominican Retreat Center in our area, where the theme was "Trust in God with all your heart." As I sat in the room with eighty other people, I realized that the retreat leaders were Father Peter and Sister Mary Ann. My heart started pounding when they called for people to give testimony to God's love in their lives. Since the time I was a little girl and watched my great-grandma Rose fervently pray the rosary, my Catholic faith had been an important part of my life. "God will provide," she often said. With this diagnosis and my ongoing issues with Brian's drinking, I found I needed and wanted my faith more than ever to strengthen and nurture my hope for our survival. The diagnosis and challenges with Brian had led me to seek a deeper understanding, one where I could lean on my faith to carry me through these dark times and try to make sense of what was happening in my life.

During the first session at the retreat center, I knew what I had to do.

My hand shot up, and I nearly jumped out of my chair before they called on me.

"I have cancer and an addicted son who is spiraling out of control," I began. "But I know God will bring me through these battles," I said, clear and certain as I continued to share all the ways God had touched my life from the moment I cried out in the emergency room until the retreat.

I was filled with a fierce belief that all would be well. In the weeks and months to come, I visualized Brian getting sober along with my own recovery. I had to take a chance—not just on myself but on my son. We were unified in the threads of our own recovery, though he wouldn't know just how much hope for his sobriety would mean for me. My deepening faith gave me the strength to believe that, one day, we'd both be healthy again.

CHAPTER 15

Hail Mary Pass, 1997

In the week that followed the diagnosis, the shortness of breath continued—and even worsened. I was fighting for my life, it seemed. The breath I had taken for granted was a life force all its own. It took minutes to walk to the bathroom. I never thought I'd collapse into my bed just after walking twenty feet from the bathroom. I was living a nightmare. Each time I fluffed the two pillows, I'd sink back into the bed as I waited for my breath to slow.

The Sunday morning after my diagnosis of Non-Hodgkin's Lymphoma was confirmed, I wanted to be alone in bed. I had assured Wayne that he could go ahead with his plans to work in the garden. *Do I dare believe that I will get better?* My thoughts turned to the phone call from my brother Gary a few days before.

"Kathy," Gary said, "Father Lubey, a priest with a healing ministry in Washington, DC, was in Corning and cured a baby with congenital heart disease who wasn't expected to live." That's all I knew about him other than Father Lubey's business card, which Gary had sent me weeks ago and that I used as a bookmark.

"Call him," he said. "I'm going to mail you the white linen handkerchief he blessed at my friend's baby's healing ceremony when he came to St. Vincent's Catholic Church, our home parish. The mother of the child gave it to me when I told her about you."

After hanging up, I pulled Father Lubey's card from my book. It had his personal phone number on the back. As I stared at it, my heart started pounding, my breath quickened, and I began praying. I stroked the card with my fingers, as if touching it would give me the strength to call. *He's probably not even at his apartment.* I scanned the room—shades pulled, clothes hanging in my closet that I didn't need at the moment, cologne and jewelry on my dresser—remnants of a life suddenly on hold. *What do I have to lose?* Wracked with uncertainty, doubt, and fear, I picked up the phone and dialed, expecting an answering machine.

After a few rings, he answered. "Hello, this is Father Lubey." The voice on the other end was gentle, and I felt an immediate relief. I had lucked out—I believe he was there for a reason, since his ministry took him around the world.

"Father," I said, "my name is Kathy. I'm from St. Vincent's in Corning, where you healed the baby. My brother gave me your name and number."

"Oh, yes," he said. "I remember. I was a vehicle for God's healing. How can I help you?"

"Father, I'm so scared," I said, holding back my tears so I could keep talking. "I've been diagnosed with Stage Four Non-Hodgkin's Lymphoma, my lungs are filled with fluid, and I can barely breathe. I don't want to die."

"Remember, you were formed in your mother's womb," he said, like a gentle prayer. "God made you special—there's no one else like you. He wants only what's best for you. He will be with you. Trust in God with all your heart, and consider yourself healed."

Like a soothing balm, his words washed over me. My tears flowed. I had no words except, "Thank you, Father."

"God bless you, child."

The warmth surged through my body in that moment and left me with a strong sense that all would be well.

After hanging up, I sat in silence and closed my eyes, allowing myself to soak up the loving presence of this holy man, whom I knew only by name and yet felt I had met in person. He gave me the fortitude to deal with the uncertain road ahead. I tried not to think about the appointment with the oncologist in two days. I didn't want to sabotage this holy man's intention for my healing.

But the stark reality of the disease remained. Each time my lungs continued to fill up with fluid, my breathing worsened. And by the time I went to the doctor's office for outpatient treatment two days after my call to Fr. Lubey, I couldn't tolerate any activity and had to use a wheelchair.

I had never felt so incapacitated in my life.

"I took one look at you and knew you were in trouble," my nurse, Diane, said, rushing me back to the treatment area and putting a nasal tube over my head to give me oxygen.

The oxygen gave me immediate relief, and my chemotherapy was initiated. As I looked up at the bag and tubing carrying the medication into my body, I thought of Father Lubey's blessing. I imagined the cancer dissolving. The more I leaned into this visualization, the easier the breathing became. Sometimes it seemed to me that the tests you endure gift you with deeper clarity and courage you never anticipated. Maybe because you are tuning into what's really important in light of a life-changing moment or event. As the mother of an addicted child, I had been prone to visualizing negative outcomes when trying to manage Brian's behavior. But now I had the opportunity to reroute that course and change my trajectory. This exercise was one of those moments that reminded me not to take life for granted. Every breath was vital.

My strong desire to live and my faith, which I believe fostered my deep connection with Father Lubey, gave me the strength to reclaim my life.

I would later read more about Father Lubey's healing ministry in his book *In the Name of Jesus, Be At Peace.* He included testimonies from people all over the world—the United States, Korea, Mexico—whom he had blessed and healed. How privileged to reach him in that moment of desperation and add my name to the long list of testimonies to his gift of healing.

CHAPTER 16

Simultaneous Battles Rage On, 1997

Having cancer did not shield me from dealing with Brian's addiction. If anything, it made me feel more vulnerable to his pleas. I was still receiving outpatient chemotherapy, and my symptoms of shortness of breath were abating.

While living at the motel we dropped him off at in February of 1977, Brian called Joe, one of the guys he'd met at the halfway house. After a few weeks, he made arrangements to move in with Joe and his girlfriend. Joe was hard-core, older, and streetwise and demanded Brian pay his rent and help with the chores. Brian complained, and initially I thought Joe might be good for him in that he set firm expectations. But I didn't trust Joe fully, and my feelings were confirmed the day toward the end of Brian's three-month stay, when Joe and Brian met me at the bank to sign off on a loan.

"Kathy, you're making a big mistake. You'll be paying off that loan," Wayne said, shaking his head in frustration.

"But Brian needs my help. I have a feeling he's in trouble, and it scares me." I knew Wayne was right, but I felt weak-kneed and vulnerable.

I didn't know what was going on, but I sensed it was shady. *Why was it so important to get that computer?* The night before, I had started watching the movie *Good Fellas*, a story about the Mafia, and I had to turn it off after about ten minutes. It felt too close to home. *What if Joe was associated with the Mafia and Brian was getting involved?*

I called Brian that night.

"Brian, I'm not comfortable signing a loan, especially when I feel Joe has conned you into convincing me to do so. I feel like he's involved in something shady."

"Mom, I'll pay you back as soon as I can. It's no big deal."

"It is a big deal to me, especially since I don't trust what's going on with Joe."

I eventually co-signed the loan, despite the red flags, which I now can see years later were proof that I was still not strong enough in my own recovery to make a firm stand. Brian had conned me.

CHAPTER 17

Searching for Rainbows, 1997

As I continued outpatient cancer chemotherapy in June 1997, Brian moved from Joe's house into an apartment in Watervliet, near Albany, about forty miles away from us. Brian was still in communication with Joe. I was so anxious for him to get out from under Joe's influence that I agreed to meet with the landlady, Yolanda, and help him with the security deposit and first month's rent. Though this made me uncomfortable, I rationalized that Brian was trying to make a new start. He had a job interview set up with a local cab company. Every decision I had to make about Brian involved an exhaustive analysis. *Was I enabling? Will this be the time he makes it?* All I wanted to do was to support him in making a better life for himself.

What I really wanted was a fresh start for both of us. I was still undergoing outpatient chemotherapy, and the outcome was uncertain.

Yolanda was a little, round, Italian motherly type lady with a soft spot for Brian. I felt instantly consoled in her presence, imagining her watching over him from across the street and baking him Italian cookies. The slightest connection to my Italian roots offered solace and reassurance. I now had a contact person to call.

I recruited some friends, and together we brought boxes of dishes, silverware, and pots and pans to help Brian get set up. He needed some furniture, and Joe suggested he drive up and down upper-crust neighborhoods to see what furniture they'd left out on the curb. Sure enough, he found a few tables, a lamp, and a chair.

Within the first week, Brian got a job as a cab driver, working nights. But that didn't help my anxiety level, since the area was crime ridden and rundown. One early morning, a few weeks after he moved in, I was awakened from a sound sleep by a loud voice: "Mom!"

I sat straight up in bed and wondered if I was dreaming.

It gave me an eerie feeling that Brian was in trouble. *What can I do? He needs his job.* Later that day, when I spoke with him, he told me he'd had a customer that night who refused to pay for his fare. Luckily nothing bad came from it.

We set up a lunch outing for the next day. I wanted to treat him for working so hard.

Yolanda was sitting on her porch when I pulled up in my car, so I crossed the street to say hello. As soon as I sat down next to her, she said,

"Brian seems like a fine young man, but sometimes I wonder how he is doing. He seems lonely to me."

"He has his struggles," I said, not sure how much to reveal to her about his drinking. It touched me that she actually cared enough about Brian to notice.

With that, Brian came bounding from across the street, cleaned up, wearing beige cargo shorts and a white polo shirt. He looked good.

We walked around town and then stopped in a corner café for lunch, where he talked about wanting to get his life together. He talked about his plans to save some money and eventually go into the Air Force. I was relieved he was making plans for his future.

"I'll never stop believing in you, B," I said as I sat across the table from him and vowed that I would never, ever give up hope that he would get sober and make a life for himself. If I could make it to the other side of cancer, he could get to the other side of his addiction. My own survival from cancer fueled my commitment to help him in his addiction recovery.

My hair was beginning to come back from the chemotherapy, and I knew that I, too, had a way to go before I was healthy and whole.

In July, a few weeks after our luncheon, Wayne offered to take me back to Missouri, the place the kids and I had lived for three years. It was also the place I had escaped from Dan, my second husband, for fear of physical abuse. The community in Missouri had embraced us while we lived there, and I had forged many close friendships. I was thrilled to see my friends again, and yet I felt conflicted about leaving Brian.

Our two-week trip filled me with dread. *How could I make sure Brian would be OK?* I had given up any thought of control over his drinking, but now that I was convinced Brian could take care of himself for longer periods of time without my supervision and help, I had to trust in my ability to thrive. Like my own recovery, I had to trust that Brian also had the ability to thrive and make the right decisions.

The week before we left, Alan, a former friend Brian had met in AA while he lived with us in Burnt Hills, had informed me that he had just picked up Brian from the police station. Brian had been arrested for breaking a mirror in a bar. He had been drinking. My heart sank.

"I'm going to bring Brian a jar of pickles to remind him that's what his brain will turn to if he keeps drinking," Alan said as a last comment on the phone, a sad reminder of what I already knew.

When I checked in on Brian the day before we left for Missouri, my firm resolve to start letting go would soon be tested again. When no one answered my knock at the door of his apartment, I slowly opened it.

There he was, lying on a bare mattress with empty beer cans strewn around him. A half-eaten ham sandwich was on a paper plate near him. My greatest fears were confirmed.

"Brian," I said softly, leaning down to touch his shoulder. "It's Mom."

I felt nauseous at the sight of his bedraggled, alcohol-soaked body and the smell of stale beer. When he finally stirred, he looked up at me with that bloodshot, glassy-eyed gaze that sent cold chills through my body. I remembered those same eyes the first time I saw him drunk eight years before.

I had anticipated finding him hung over and had brought holy water from a friend who had visited Medjugory, the mountain village in Yugoslavia where legend has it that the Virgin Mother appeared to three children. I walked around the apartment, through each room, sprinkling the water and praying the Hail Mary, willing the holy water would protect him from the evil forces of addiction. The kitchen sink was filled with dirty, food-caked dishes, the counter with empty pizza boxes. The bedroom had piles of filthy clothes heaped on the floor.

As I performed my ritual, Brian remained in his stupor.

Finally, I knelt down and kissed his sweaty forehead. I sprinkled him with the holy water and prayed that he would stay alive long enough to get sober.

"I love you, B." He did not respond.

I left this apartment with a heavy heart. I wondered if I would see him alive after my return from Missouri. I turned to my faith: "Dear God, you'll have to watch over him. Please help him awaken to his problem, and give me the strength to let go." I wondered if I could live with myself for leaving. And yet, I also knew my staying would not save him. I would have to trust that God would take care of him, just as He'd taken care of me during my cancer treatment.

In August of 1997, a few weeks after returning from Missouri, I began having a cough and increased shortness of breath. A CT scan confirmed that the lymphoma had recurred. This time, I was hospitalized every three weeks for chemotherapy. I couldn't handle the craziness with

Brian when I already had challenges with my treatment. The diagnosis and treatment forced me to focus on myself and many times took the choice away from me when I was hospitalized for chemotherapy. Brian couldn't reach me by phone because he wouldn't know I was hospitalized. His behavior never stopped me from loving him or caring about him, but being in the hospital was an external mechanism to keep me shielded from his requests for money or sympathy for getting into the crises he created.

As a result, I would simply pray that God would keep him safe. In my prayers, I always told Brian I loved him. I did love him, more than anything. I hated the addiction and what it was doing to him. If that's what letting go meant, I was doing my best. It was not easy, but, as I'd learned in countless Al-Anon meetings, I would be helping the addiction escalate if I continued to do what he should and could do for himself. I had to break my addiction to his addiction. That didn't mean I had to to stop loving my son, nor would I.

Brian eventually moved out of his Watervliet apartment and stayed with us briefly before going into the Air Force. The November day he was to leave, he left a knotted-up sheet hanging from a pipe in the cellar. I was terrified when I saw it, but Wayne, who dismissed it as a manipulative gesture on Brian's part, said to Brian right before we drove him to the airport, "Make sure you do it right, so I don't have a mess to clean up."

I cringed at his statement. Though I was beginning to see Brian's pattern of manipulation more clearly, I still carried a nagging worry with me. I knew we were risking an opportunity to truly support Brian. He could have accidentally killed himself, or he could have meant it and followed through. Years later, he confided a real suicide attempt while living in the Watervliet apartment before he left for the Air Force.

"One day, I tried to hang myself with a sheet, but the sheet unraveled just in time," he said during a family session in one of his rehab programs.

"I blacked out momentarily and started coughing. When I looked around my apartment, I realized how close I'd come. I didn't want to die."

If I had known that at the time, I would have had an even harder time letting him go. I had to rely on my faith, Al-Anon meetings, and living one day at a time to get through these agonizing moments of uncertainty.

But I was also weary of his non-stop manipulations and lies. I couldn't get him on that plane fast enough. Even though I questioned if he was ready, I knew he needed structure. I prayed the experience would give him what he needed. His dad, Ed, and stepmom Jean met us at the airport to bid Brian farewell. As we watched him board his plane for San Antonio, I think we all breathed a sigh of relief. The blank stare on Brian's face scared me to death.

Over the next few months, while I was undergoing chemotherapy treatments and traveling back and forth to Boston for an evaluation for a stem-cell transplant, Brian was going through basic training in San Antonio, Texas. Every day that went by without any bad news, from either my doctors or from San Antonio, felt like a reprieve. A recent CT scan would reveal if I was in remission, and, if so, I would qualify for a stem-cell transplant in Boston. I awaited news of the results.

On my way back from Mass one cloudy, cool November Sunday morning, I stopped at a red light with thoughts of my CT scan results and Brian bouncing around in my head. *Will I be in remission? Will Brian recover? Please, Lord—give me strength.*

As I looked up at the gray sky, a rainbow peeked out from the dark clouds. I smiled as a sense of hope washed over me. Within a few days, my doctor called me to declare that I was in remission from cancer, and Brian called from San Antonio to tell me he'd been assigned to Eielson Air Force Base in Fairbanks, Alaska. I was on my way to Boston for a stem-cell transplant, and Brian was on his way to the last frontier to establish a career in the Air Force.

A new chapter began.

CHAPTER 18

River of Time, 1998

Fear and negative thinking had been my way of controlling my response to Brian's drinking. If I expected the worst, then I wouldn't be surprised when the outcomes were not what I wanted them to be. But I knew this wasn't going to work in my battle with cancer. I had to maintain a positive attitude and fighting spirit. After two years of chemotherapy and radiation treatments, I finally qualified for a peripheral stem-cell transplant at New England Medical Center in Boston. It was my shot at a cure, described as an insurance policy. My stem cells (forerunner of all blood cells found in the bone marrow) would be collected and re-infused back to my bone marrow (the birthplace for all blood cells) and begin producing new blood cells. I would be in isolation at the hospital, as the high-dose chemotherapy before the procedure would kill my bone marrow. When the stem cells were infused back into me, they'd go right to the bone marrow and begin producing new blood cells. The idea was to kill any cancer-producing blood cells and start fresh with new cells. I would be in the hospital for one month.

As I watched from the eighth-floor window of the New England Medical Center how the Boston morning traffic inched through the Big Dig—what felt like a never-ending megaproject of rerouting the traffic in and around Boston from 1991 to 2006—the traffic flowed like a river. But in this "river," everyone appeared to be in such a hurry. What were all those hurried, harried people thinking? Were they grateful for their lives and blessings or obsessing over trivial, insignificant details as they endlessly traipsed through all the minutiae of day-to-day life?

And yet, here I was in 1998, at fifty-two years old and not ready to die from Stage Four Non-Hodgkin's Lymphoma. Each day felt like a caterpillar as I inched my way through the daily hospital routine before my stem-cell transplant. Multiple cycles of outpatient chemotherapy had finally put me in remission in November 1997. Just when I thought I was cured, the cardiologist at New England Medical Center told me during a pre-procedure consultation a few weeks before my admission that I might not survive the stem-cell procedure due to heart damage from the previous chemotherapy.

As I lay in my hospital bed, following the slow drip of the medicine in the IV chamber, I wondered if the lymphoma would come back—now a reality in my life. I waged a mental, spiritual, emotional, and physical battle against fear and negative thinking of—I don't know what: loss of control? And yet that fear and negative thinking were keeping me small, unable to live my deepest potential. It was time to change the channel on this way of thinking. I was reaching for a level of acceptance that would enable me to live my life to the fullest. Cancer wasn't mine. I did not claim it. And yet I was the cancer patient in Room #8031, or, to put it more humanely, the person in #8031 with a cancer diagnosis. I was Medical Record #181-81-94. The IVs were flowing, the orders were written, and all other plans were on hold—the new job, my wedding, life as I knew it. But I was still a woman, a mother, a lover, a daughter, a sister, a niece, an aunt, a cousin, a friend, a colleague, a nurse, and a teacher.

Doctors insisted I could be cured, and I put my hopes into this stem-cell transplant.

I willed myself to believe in my ability to get through this as I returned to the bed, guiding the pole with bags of fluid hanging from multiple hooks—a scene I knew well from my years of caring for others. I vowed to fight my way to the other side of cancer and past getting caught up in the unimportant things, just as I imagined was the case with the drivers eight floors below, sitting in gridlock.

I was once one of those hurried, harried people rushing to get somewhere, to get it all done, with a knot in my gut and a constant anxiety in my mind and heart. I wish I didn't have to go back there, but I wanted to get on with my life with a newfound sense of clarity, appreciation, and priorities. As I reflect on this moment now, I wondered how it was possible to move on even when I was forced to let go of control as I was constantly challenged to do with Brian and his drinking.

My cancer diagnosis made me realize that any sense of control was an illusion.

But as difficult as it was to let go of my own mortality, nothing could compare with witnessing how my son was destroying his own life with alcohol. At least I could combat my disease with medications and procedures. But while I was a fighter, Brian was one drink away from drinking his way out of life. Even though he was doing well, his sobriety was uncertain.

Presently, Dr. Steinbach and his crew of residents and interns, dressed in Mickey Mouse ties, entered, smiling. They made me laugh and gave me hope—I will survive and go on to see better days. They reviewed my upcoming procedure, which would take place in my hospital room in three days; then I would recover for one month in the hospital. Then they warned me that the odor of fish will permeate the room while my stem cells were being infused back into me. Interesting, but I never asked why.

"Let the games begin," I said, and they smiled and nodded their heads.

For the next three days, the battle of my life and for my life raged on, and, the more entrenched I got, thinking positive thoughts, the closer to God I felt. His presence sustained and strengthened me. I relied on my faith for the hope and strength I knew I would need for the battles ahead.

On Ash Wednesday, 1998, I was admitted to the hospital where I would begin my forty days in the desert before walking the road to Calvary with my savior, Jesus Christ. I looked over at the tubing and followed it to the port-a-cath imbedded in my right-upper chest. I visualized the lifeblood of Christ flowing through my veins. At that moment, I gave myself permission to let go. There was nothing else to do.

River of time, keep flowing onward. Let the healing begin.

PART III

Breaking the Cycle

You tell me that recovery is starting over, like a flower ready to bud.

Caught in the web of my own self-defeating, enabling patterns, I must break free and fly on the wave of hope . . .

May I live and let live. I don't have to be in charge of everything. My son is capable, and he is the only one who can determine his path.

Let him go in peace and live in the peace of knowing you love him and believe in him.

~ Personal journal entry

CHAPTER 19

Setting Boundaries, 1999–2001

During the two years of cancer treatment and one year after the stem-cell transplant, I slowly accepted that learning to do less for Brian would force him to take personal responsibility. In 1999, one year after Brian entered the Air Force, we spoke frequently on the phone while he was stationed at Eielson Air Force Base in Fairbanks, Alaska, and he often expressed his discontent with being in Alaska. He sounded lonely and depressed, and I feared he was isolating himself. I couldn't imagine facing hours of darkness and feeling alone in the vast Alaskan wilderness. My heart broke, sensing the wide distances that separated us. I wondered if he was turning to drinking to cope with his loneliness.

My worst fears were confirmed six months later in that summer of 1999, when I received a phone call from his commanding officer that Brian had missed work and would be attending an alcohol-rehab program at Travis Air Force Base in California when he missed work. I felt immediate relief that he was getting help, yet a deep sadness that drinking still had a hold on him. Leigh was on summer break from grad school, and she and I had traveled cross-country to attend the family program before his discharge. Since we went by way of military medical transport, we were at the mercy of the military's schedule and ended up puddle-jumping across the country from base to base—thirty-three takeoffs and landings from Syracuse to northern California, near Sacramento.

With each new crew, Leigh Ann and I were questioned.

The flight attendant asked us, "When was your last drink?"

At first, we looked at each other in puzzlement, but eventually we figured out it was because we were attending the family program for alcohol rehabilitation. *No—we aren't the problem drinkers.*

Since I was considered the patient due to the transplant and resulting health issue of congestive heart failure, the nurse on each flight took my vital signs. By the time we arrived in California, we were exhausted from the frequent landings, takeoffs, and sleeping at different bases during the thirty-six-hour trip. At one point, while taking our luggage to our room at Dover Air Base in Delaware, out of sheer exasperation, Leigh Ann announced,

"I'm taking a bus back home." She looked straight at me, resolute, eyes blazing, face flushed.

What can I say? I thought. Her presence would be important to Brian, and yet I knew their relationship was tentative, fueled by years of his drinking and disruptive behavior. It was a huge commitment to take time off from her summer job and accompany me. I also needed her support as I was still feeling the effects of the stem-cell transplant, mostly decreased stamina and shortness of breath with activity. The success of the transplant would be revealed over time. I was still in the waiting period. The trip was a strain on my compromised body, but my mother's heart led the way. I wanted Leigh Ann to have the opportunity to share her concerns about Brian's drinking. My greatest wish is that they would gain a better understanding of each other and that we all three would learn and grow from the experience.

I listened to her pleas to be free of all the chaos surrounding her brother, and then I said,

"Leigh, I understand. This has been a difficult trip. I know you have been through hell with your brother. I hope you'll give it some more thought before you leave. Both Brian and I need you to be a part of this."

I hoped that expressing her feelings and a little time might help her gain some perspective. We walked to the cafeteria and ate dinner in silence. On our way back to our room, she turned to me and said,

"I'm OK, Mom."

I held out my arms and wrapped her in a big hug. It relieved me to know she would continue to support me in our travels.

"Good, honey. We need you."

Addiction breaks hearts and forces one to examine boundaries with the person who is drinking. It affects every single member of a family. The three of us were all in need of healing, and I held out expectations that this program would help us break through the silence and shame and start living in a healthy way.

After thirty-six hours of non-stop travel, we finally met up with Brian, who looked rested and humbled. We stayed for a week, attending sessions and immersing ourselves in our collective recovery. The three of us took one day to ride the ferry to San Francisco and walk Fisherman's Wharf. It turned out to be too much for me physically, as I experienced increased fatigue and shortness of breath. We went directly to the emergency department from the ferry on our return, and I was diagnosed with an episode of congestive heart failure, but luckily it was reversed effectively with medications.

Brian had done well in the program, and I had every reason to believe he would stay committed to it. Yet, doubts and fears surfaced on the last night we were there. Several of the program participants were caught leaving the premises and drinking alcohol. I breathed a sigh of relief that Brian was not among them, but I worried about how he would do once he got back to his base. *Would he be strong enough to maintain sobriety? Would he isolate himself and fall back into old patterns?* The realization that there was no quick fix and that recovery takes a concerted effort every day was sobering to me. I had already learned that a few weeks in rehab was no guarantee that sobriety would be maintained.

In December, five months after he was discharged from the rehab program, I received an unexpected phone call at work.

"Brian has a drinking problem," the commanding officer at Eielson Air Force Base said on the phone. "I saw what he could do when he was sober. We're discharging him under honorable conditions so he can receive medical benefits."

My son had been in the service for two years.

"What happened?" I asked.

"When he didn't show up for work, we went to his room and found him hung over, still garbling his words and acting argumentative."

"He was doing so well," I said, recalling the trip to Alaska Leigh Ann and I had taken a year ago.

"Yes, he was, especially after we sent him to Travis Air Force Base for rehab. I have a brother who is an alcoholic. It's a disease."

"Thank you, officer," I said, my heart in my throat. "I appreciate your generosity in giving Brian medical benefits. I know he will need them."

The peace I felt about Brian being in the Air Force and establishing himself on a career path was shattered. I was hoping that the service would give him much-needed structure, and now that he was out of the Air Force, I was worried. I began to realize that the structure I anticipated would help Brian was an illusion.

He would be flying home. Where would he live? What would he do? Would he be open to getting the help he needed? He would have to stay with Wayne and me in Burnt Hills until he figured things out. Although I continued to take responsibility for Brian for his actions, the thought of him coming back home terrified me. Al-Anon continued to be my lifeline, as it had been since 1996, as I brought my fears and worries to the meetings and waited for the next crisis.

He arrived Christmas Eve, 1999, a week after the officer called me. He stayed with us through the Christmas holiday. As I looked into his hollow eyes and watched him pacing and bolting out the door, the Brian I still knew was in need of ongoing treatment, but he made no attempt to go to AA meetings or get a sponsor despite my pleas. Soon after he moved back with us, he decided to drive to Connecticut.

"Connecticut? What's in Connecticut?"

"I want to walk around Yale and sit in on a few classes. Explore my options."

He took off just like that without giving thought to his action. He rented a car with money left over from the service and took off, doing it his way. So, when he left for Connecticut in January 2000, a few weeks after returning home, my heart felt like a stone in my throat as I waited in torment the seventy-two hours until his return.

The car was due back three days later, on Friday at 4:00 p.m., and Brian was nowhere in sight.

At 9:00 p.m., I received a phone call from one of Brian's high school friends, Don, who worked at TGIF Fridays in a nearby town.

"Brian's getting drunk at the bar."

Wayne and I drove the twenty miles to the restaurant. I stormed into the restaurant, went up to the bar, and glared at him as he stood there joking with the bartender.

"We're here to pick you up," I said, wanting to shake him. *How humiliating for a grown man to have his mother come after him, yet what choice did I have?* At that moment, my anger, fueled by fear—fear that he would attempt to drive home and crash—took over.

"Mom, it's not what you think. I had a great trip and sat in on a class at Yale."

He didn't look drunk. His words weren't slurred, and he looked casual and comfortable as he described his trip. *Maybe his tolerance was increasing, another sign of the addiction progressing.*

"Your car was due back at 4:00 p.m. today, and you'll be paying a late fee."

I was in no mood for a social chat. I wish I could have been excited for him, but I knew his drinking was ruling his life, and, until he admitted it and decided to make the necessary changes, I was powerless.

"Come home—now," I said, not knowing if he would resist.

He put his drink down, zipped up his coat, and followed me out the door.

After months of continuing in this way, he eventually crashed and ended up in detox in Connecticut—where he'd moved shortly after the incident at Fridays—too many times to count. Sometimes he ended up in another alcohol-rehabilitation program. He always made sure to call me each time. I felt like I was his lifeline. I didn't know if he had any friends. While in Connecticut in a halfway house in 2000, he started seeing a psychologist, Dr. Gill, who seemed to understand and like Brian. He did well and even spoke at Alcoholic Anonymous (AA) about his journey to sobriety. When he followed the AA program of attending meetings and getting a sponsor, he was able to stay sober. Structure and accountability were the hallmarks of the program.

When Wayne and I announced our wedding plans for October 2001, it was such a thrill to see Brian achieve the sobriety I always thought in my heart he could achieve. Living within the defined boundaries of recovery, we both experienced a sense of newfound freedom. But his recovery followed suit with what was predicted of anyone in recovery—alternating periods of sobriety and relapses. Relapse, I was told, was part of recovery. I continued to attend Al-Anon meetings and work on my own recovery from co-dependence one day at a time. As much as I embraced his sobriety, I knew it was tenuous and that the slightest slip could change everything again—and the feeling of navigating this rocky road was similar to climbing a mountain.

"We're in this together, B," I said to him during one of his sober visits a few weeks before our wedding day. "It feels so good to have you back."

"It's great to be back, Mom."

I hung on to the sense that we were moving forward as mother and son in a healthy way.

He had secured a job at J.C. Penney's, in the business office, bought a used car, and attended college at the University of Bridgeport while living in the halfway house. During his first semester, in 2000, he played on the college baseball team and maintained a 4.0 cumulative GPA in his general studies. Hope was running high again, although I knew I had to temper my hope with the reality that relapse was likely until he fully committed to making his sobriety a priority every day. I, too, had to learn to take one day at a time.

A cool, crisp morning with brilliant oranges and reds marked my wedding day—October 27, 2001—and the beginning of a life of love worth waiting for. Wayne and I had each traveled a rocky, tortuous road—through divorces, single parenting, troubled sons—to find each other. I rode to the church in the back seat of Uncle Michael's Cadillac. One hundred and fifty family and friends packed Our Lady of Grace Catholic Church. Dad had suffered a bout of atrial fibrillation and required a cardioversion (electrical shock) procedure and the insertion of a pacemaker three weeks before the wedding. But on that day, he was strong and proud as he walked me down the aisle. I was fifty-five years old, and the joyous feeling of getting married for the "first time" swept over me. I think we both realized this was the real thing as he leaned over to kiss me when we reached Wayne and Father Tony. I saw a small tear roll down Dad's cheek. It felt like nothing was going to stop the joy and happiness.

My heart, already bursting with happiness about marrying Wayne, was filled with hope that the change in Brian would be a lasting one. Wayne stood quietly in the background, holding his breath. His calm demeanor was an effective counterbalance to my frazzled, emotion-filled nature when it came to my son.

My clear-eyed, sober son read from Corinthians about faith, hope, and love at our wedding Mass on October 27, 2001—six weeks after 9/11 when the world stood still and life changed forever for all of us and the entire world at large. I was hopeful that our marriage was the beginning of a new, sober life for my son and a return to some peace and sanity in our lives. My parents and Wayne had witnessed Brian's erratic behavior over the years and had voiced concern over my safety and peace of mind. Wayne saw more than they did and made it clear that Brian needed limits. I soaked up the reprieve from all the angst and chose to enjoy each moment of this one precious day.

When Brian reached the podium for the first scripture reading, people took note of that tall, handsome young man and his ability to read with such passion and charisma. My relatives didn't really know Brian, as he had been absent from so many family gatherings for years, and so his presence marked a sea change of sorts.

"My gosh," Dad's sister, my Aunt Ruth, said, "he is a fine young man."

Yes, I thought, Brian is showing himself as the passionate, sensitive young man I always believed him to be underneath the shackles of his drinking. I soaked in that moment as my validation that I had every reason to hope in his sobriety.

With our six children surrounding us on the altar—Wayne's four children and their spouses, Leigh, Brian, my nieces, Carly and Annie, and Carly's seeing-eye dog, Amber—Father Tony pronounced us man and wife. We were officially a family before God and our family and friends. What joy I felt standing next to my husband as a feeling of getting married for the "first time" washed over me. I was hopeful that Brian was feeling a part of our growing circle of love and that this would make a difference in helping him achieve long-term sobriety.

At the reception, Brian and I danced the Mother-and-Son dance. I looked up into his clear, bright eyes and recalled the very first moment I held him as a newborn and fell in love with him—my son with so much promise.

CHAPTER 20

A Bird Who Can't Fly, 2002

About six months after our wedding, Brian relapsed. He stayed in the halfway house in Connecticut during this time and gave every indication that he was maintaining his sobriety, calling me regularly and even visiting us a few times.

"Mom, I'm ready to move on," he said, adding that he needed help with the security deposit on a new apartment. My uneasy feelings should have been sufficient warning to hold off on handing over the money to his landlord. I was still quite vulnerable to his pleas, feeling the weight of past relapses.

"I met with a person who is looking for a roommate to help with expenses," he said one day toward the end of his stay in the halfway house. "It's a woman."

"Are you sure you can handle living with a young woman, B?" I said. By this time, my heart was in my throat, imagining all sorts of scenarios that would not be in his best interest. As far as I knew, Brian did not have a girlfriend or date. At least he never mentioned it. His drinking took precedence, and, when he drank, he had no money to spend on girls.

"It's not what you think," he said. "She has a full-time job for a phone company, and I'm in school. We have our own lives."

"How am I supposed to trust that you can go from a halfway house with structure to living with a strange woman? It seems pretty drastic to me."

"Well, don't you think you should start trusting me?" he said. "I've been sober for more than a year, and I had a great first semester."

"I know, B," I said, "and I'm proud of you for how far you've come."

By the time that phone call was over, I felt torn. On one hand, I rationalized that he proved he could handle a year of sobriety and convinced myself that he deserved a chance to succeed. On the other hand, I made myself crazy trying to figure out if I should help him. His relapses made it difficult for me to trust him. *Is this the time I can trust him? Will I be hurting him by helping him? Is the real Brian back, or is the addiction still lurking close by?* For some reason, I reluctantly agreed to pay for his security deposit and first month's rent directly to the landlord. I knew it was against my better judgment, but, at that point, I was not able to set a firm boundary and refuse to pay.

Two weeks later, initial reports were glowing when Brian moved into the apartment. He met with Louise ahead of time and apparently made a good impression, as she didn't hesitate to invite him to be her roommate.

"He's a perfect gentleman," she chirped one day during his first week there, when I called to talk to Brian. I hung on to hope that I could keep trusting Brian, although I had learned to keep my enthusiasm at bay. I decided not to say anything about Brian's drinking to Louise, to let the situation play out. I wondered what Louise looked like, how old she was. Mostly I wondered how Brian was handling a roommate relationship with a woman, since, as far as I knew, he hadn't dated for a while.

However, within a matter of days after I talked with Louise, frantic phone calls from Brian, his pressured speech, laced with anger toward others, including Louise. A sense of dread washed over me with each call. The combination of fear and anger left me feeling weak. Defeated. I worried about how Brian's behavior was affecting Louise.

"Mom, the guys on the baseball team are acting weird toward me," he said, his voice urgent and fast-paced. "I don't know what I have done." I had no idea what he was talking about and wondered if his paranoia was an indicator that he had started drinking again.

Before I could ask any questions, he tried to reassure me, "I'm alright, Mom. I'll be fine."

With that, I knew he wasn't fine, and I braced myself. The fact that I had contributed to his relapse since I had subsidized his rent triggered feelings of guilt and helplessness.

My worst fears of him relapsing outside the structure of a halfway house were confirmed when Louise called in tears the day after Brian called me. He had given her my phone number. I realized I was his only support. I wished he had friends close by to turn to. As I look back, I now realize that I had nurtured that dependence on me by always being there for him and in many cases by bailing him out. It was a hard line for a mother to walk. *How do I keep loving my son but not enabling his dependent behavior?*

"He's crazy," Louise said as she sobbed into the phone two weeks after he had moved in.

"Louise, what's going on?" I asked, with dread, my heart pounding.

"He started acting funny—shouting like he was angry at someone," she said. "He scares me."

"Go on," I said, visualizing my 6'1" son with flashing eyes and a flushed face, spewing his anger in this girl's home. Of course, she was scared. Alcohol always turned him into someone I would not want to run into.

"Two weeks ago, we were making dinner together and having a great time. I almost thought it was too good to be true," she said during one phone conversation after he started drinking.

"I'm so sorry you had to experience this, Louise," I said. "He must have started drinking again." I wanted to scream.

"Yes," she said. Then she added, "I had to call my brother to kick Brian out. He took off and was arrested for driving under the influence (DUI) and for disturbing the peace two days later. I have a restraining order against him because he scares me. I've never seen anyone change as fast as he did," she said. "He went from a perfect gentleman to a monster in a matter of a week."

I felt sickened and heartbroken when I heard her words. A deep sense of loss enveloped me as I faced the stark reality—I would need to figure out a way to let go of my son, who was defined by the disease of addiction.

One month into the second semester in 2002, the University of Bridgeport newspaper spelled out the truth about my son in bold, undeniable print. Just below the announcement of Brian's placement on the President's List of scholar-athletes of the Fall semester was the article about Brian and another student being charged with marijuana possession.

Wayne and I braced ourselves for the calamity of another relapse; we wondered how much further down he could dig himself and if he would survive this time.

The week after Brian left her apartment, Louise kept in touch frequently. The painful details were almost too much to bear.

"I changed the lock for fear that Brian would try to break in one day."

"I threw his clothes out the window when he showed up outside one day."

"He must have a wet brain from all the drinking because he acts crazy."

After hearing these things from someone whom I once thought was Brian's friend reinforced my underlying lack of trust that had haunted me ever since Brian had started drinking, at the age of fourteen.

The following week, I made arrangements to have all his belongings in Louise's apartment packed up and delivered to our home. I offered to pay for the U-Haul, and Louise and her brother drove 200 miles to our home to drop off furniture, clothes, and papers. The remnants of his tattered life sat sadly in our garage, but doing this reminded me how I kept doing for him what he should be doing for himself. Once again, I felt "had" by him, manipulated into picking up his pieces. But there were no other options. Like Brian, I needed support and help and looked to Al-Anon meetings to get me through as it had for the past six years.

During that cold, gray February day in 2002, while waiting for Louise and her brother, I wondered how many more relapses it would take for Brian to take personal responsibility. I feared for his life. Just then, I received a phone call from Brian. He was staying at the Fenway Park Hotel. He started ranting about Satan being in the room. "I want to beat Satan up, Mom," he said in escalating, panicky tones.

I held the receiver to my ear, helpless, panic-stricken. Having heard these religious rants before when he had been drinking, I braced myself for the chaos that usually followed. After a few endless seconds, I found the words.

"Brian, I'm going to keep praying right now. Dear Lord, please watch over Brian and banish Satan in your name," I prayed, followed by the Our Father and Hail Mary.

With that, he started sobbing. Then he said, "I'm OK, Mom. Gotta' go," and hung up. The fear of that situation rattled me. I was terrified for him and could only imagine how terrified he must have been.

Fifteen minutes later, Louise and her brother arrived with Brian's belongings, and, at the same time, the hotel manager phoned to say that Brian had torn up the room and was heard screaming and throwing things. An ambulance had been called, and he'd been transported to the emergency room for a psychiatric evaluation. I decided not to say anything to Louise, but the fear for Brian's life paralyzed me. Louise had been through enough, and I didn't want to keep dragging her into the fray. I also didn't want to talk about it. My sense of trust had been battered, ruptured.

Together we unloaded the truck, and I invited Louise and her brother to join Wayne, Leigh Ann, and myself for dinner. We ate in silence, pulled down by waves of discomfort and sadness, realizing at that moment that the good feelings Louise had initially experienced with Brian had now been obscured by this series of events. I wanted to hang on to those good memories and believe that Brian would return again—healthy, whole, and sober.

After Wayne and Leigh Ann cleared the dishes, I was fueled by a deep need to reassure myself that I wasn't about to lose my son. I wanted everyone—Louise, Leigh Ann, Wayne—to know that my son wasn't a menace to society. That he was actually a sensitive, caring person with a disease, and he needed help.

"Louise, let me show you something." I motioned her into the guest bedroom after dinner.

As we walked through the door, I pointed to the collage on the dresser of our wedding, with photos of a bright young man smiling and dancing with his mother.

"This is the Brian I know and love. I know he needs help, but I will never, ever give up hope that he will come back."

"I hope you're right," Louise said, shaking her head. "I really do."

Her downward glance and furrowed brow told me she wasn't buying my optimism. I sensed she had his best interest at heart and was genuinely concerned. She had seen the Brian I saw and watched him self-destruct. Though her response was disappointing, I understood why she was wary. I also resolved to dig my heels in deeper and keep believing with all my heart that my son would find his way out of this big, black hole of addiction.

Once Louise and her brother drove off, I felt at liberty to absorb the grief and sorrow about Brian's relapse. I walked Leigh Ann out to her car and slid into the front seat, where we both lingered in the aftermath of the grief and sorrow.

"Mom, it's up to him," Leigh Ann said. "He's the only one who can decide to change."

My heart was heavy.

"I know, honey. I know," I said, soaking up the wisdom of my twenty-something daughter, a wisdom beyond her years.

Addiction has a nasty way of making you feel like the one you love is no longer emotionally present, but on that night, Leigh Ann and I both made a conscious effort to connect to the "pure" image of Brian—the one we knew in our hearts still existed underneath the addiction. A clean, sober, vivacious Brian. We talked about the good times when he was sober—my wedding day, when he'd lit up the room with his presence, his twenty-first birthday, when he pulled up in his new car, a used BMW, our trip to Fairbanks, Alaska, when he was stationed at Eielson Air Force Base; our visit to California a year later in 1999, when he was sent for alcohol rehabilitation at Travis Air Force Base near Sacramento, and we shared in his recovery.

"Mom," Leigh Ann said, "that's why I wrote that poem about him."

"Yes, 'A Bird Who Can't Fly.' I remember," I said. "We were at the closing session of the family program at Travis Air Force Base in California."

After he received his gold coin etched with the Serenity Prayer, Brian came back to join us in the audience. I was overjoyed to have my clear-eyed, handsome son back. As we stood up to get some refreshments, Brian wrapped Leigh Ann and me in a big bear hug that I wanted to last forever.

"I have something for you, B," Leigh Ann said and handed him a framed poem she had written him during our time at Travis.

I could not treat Brian like I treated Leigh Ann. While I respected her right to live her life because I trusted her, she was angry at her brother, but still she found a way to express her love for him in this poem she wrote:

A Bird Who Cannot Fly

I think of you as a bird who can't fly,
As if you're afraid of the sky but I don't know why.
You have all the ingredients to learn how to soar,
But the choices you made sent you through the wrong door.
What you need to find is the courage to win,
But you must find your own courage and find it within.
There are obstacles in life you must overcome,

And tough times ahead are far from being done.
It's time for you to open your eyes
And look at yourself as a bird who CAN fly.

After he read it, blinking back tears, he said, "Wow, Leigh-Leigh, this is amazing." I think he really felt his sister's love at that moment—that she believed in his ability to succeed.

We stood in silence during that Alaska visit, soaking up what felt like a loving moment. I would cherish that moment forever.

When we boarded our plane to return home from Alaska a few days later, my hard-earned sense of calm and hope from attending the family rehabilitation program over the last few days teetered. In the moment I waved goodbye to my sober son, I could see how, from a distance, he managed to wipe a tear from his eye. It suddenly appeared how fragile and emotional he had become. My son. *Will he be able to sustain his sobriety in this vast wilderness?* I had to be strong and hopeful for us both. The bonding effect of witnessing the immense beauty of Alaska's expansive wilderness over land and sea matched the unfolding of our bonding over the last few days. *Could it be that the landscape brought out the best in Brian?* At every tour stop, I had every reason to hope that Brian would be alright. Our visit was a taste of how I wanted it to be and—in my mind—how it should be.

Alaska's expansive wilderness also matched my own emotional wilderness. I was afraid to enter unknown territory, and, worse, beyond all, I was afraid to leave my son behind to fend for himself. I carried that teardrop with me like excess baggage, securely packed away in my mind and heart.

It was time to go. I leaned over to hug Leigh Ann, grateful for her companionship during what felt like a very trying time. I wished I could wash away the years of hurt, but now we needed to be emotionally available for each other. Her grief and hurt were different from mine. Like me, she was heartbroken and scared for Brian's welfare, but she had to contend with years of anger for putting up with his behavior. She had always been fond of him, but she needed to protect herself and had learned to set healthy boundaries with him, calling him out when he needed it and refusing to be manipulated by him. *What more did we have in that moment but the memories of good times and the hope for better times?* It hurt me that Leigh Ann felt so distant from her brother, but I understood. It takes two people to nurture a relationship. Her love and concern for her brother came through in her poem.

"Be strong, Mom," she said. "You're doing everything you can." Her response surprised me because, in fact, I should be the one supporting her. Clearly, she had gotten past feeling like a victim and wanted me to feel encouraged and supported.

"Please don't give up on your brother," I said.

"I won't, Mom."

I slid out of Leigh's car and walked back to the house, filled with hope that Brian would survive.

The phone was ringing when I opened the front door, and my heart leaped in my chest. *Maybe it's Brian?*

"Ma'am, are you the mother of Brian?"

Oh, my God. I pray he's alive.

"Yes, I am."

"This is Doctor Sullivan from Boston General emergency department."

I felt lightheaded and had to sit down.

"We have your son, Brian, here, basically sleeping off a binge. He'll be discharged as soon as he sobers up."

"Oh, please—don't discharge him. He needs help," I said.

"I understand your concern, but my hands are tied. I can't keep him against his will. He should be ready to be released in a few hours."

With that, I braced myself for more chaos and phone calls.

At 1:00 a.m. the following morning, Brian called from a train station in Boston, followed by a frantic call 10 hours later from Grand Central Station in New York City.

"Hey, Mom. Guess where I am," he asked, like he was proud of his escapade.

"Brian, it's one o'clock the morning," I said, still groggy from being awakened from a sound sleep. I wanted to vomit. He was spiraling out of control, which led me to hang on in an attempt to steady myself.

Episodic nights, wondering if Brian was dead or alive, had plagued me since 1990, the first time I saw Brian drunk.

That same night, after he had been discharged from the emergency room, he called from Grand Central Station.

"I sold my car and some of my belongings and got a train ticket," he said. "I want to go back to Connecticut.

"Mom, I just kept praying the Hail Mary over and over when I arrived at the station." It eased my frantic mind to know he could pray in times of need.

"Brian, please get help when you get to Connecticut," I said. "Look up Dr. Gill."

"I love you, B."

"Love you, too, Mom."

CHAPTER 21

Choices and Chances, 2002

After Brian's last phone call, in desperation, I opened up in Al-Anon meetings, which I attended two to three times a week. Battle-scarred veterans listened and consoled. They helped me navigate the minefields of living with and loving an alcoholic.

"You have control only over yourself, Kathy," the group leader said, sitting erect in her seat. Her perfectly coifed blond hair and neatly trimmed, painted nails gave her an air of control and confidence.

"You never stop loving them, but you can't do for Brian what he can and should be doing for himself," said an elderly lady across the table from me, nodding her head.

"I love him," I said. "But I hate his behavior when he drinks. How can I reconcile the two?"

"You have to be strong, or you'll go down with him."

"I'm afraid he's going to die one of these times," I said, grabbing more tissues.

"He may, but there is nothing you can do about it. You must concentrate on yourself."

I railed against this logic. "No, you can't tell me I can just let go and be done with him." I looked down at my lap and wrung my hands as I listened to their advice.

The room went silent, but when I looked up, I saw the faces of mothers, fathers, lovers who carried the same pain I was carrying. They knew the heartache and the frustrations of loving an addict. They hugged me with their soft glances and nods; then one man, worn down from his own battle with an addicted son, spoke softly,

"Sometimes all we can do for our loved one is pray."

With that, we held hands and chanted the mantra that ended every meeting: "Keep coming back. It works if you work it."

It was then that I realized I had found a family—others who truly understood my pain. Nobody could understand the terror of loving an addict—not even my own flesh-and-blood family, who'd never experienced addiction—as much as these fellow travelers. Hugs and tears would get me through another day.

After many unsuccessful attempts to stand firm and set limits with Brian, I found my courage one snowy March night in 2002.

On that night, Wayne and I were awakened by a loud knocking at the front door at 2:00 a.m. We forced ourselves out of bed and looked at each other. Wayne followed close behind me. Through the front-door window, I saw Brian's tall, dark outline against the soft, fluffy flakes of snow that had coated the trees and roofs.

As I opened the door, I looked into his eyes. They always told me the true story about whether he was drinking or not. He shot me a dull and distant stare. Not a good sign. He stepped inside, rubbed his hands down his pant legs, and cleared his throat. He was neatly groomed in jeans, a sweater, and a navy pea coat. He smelled of Hugo Boss cologne. His eyes were glassy as he shifted his gaze.

"Hey, Mom."

When he ignored Wayne, I realized something was wrong. He greeted me casually as if he had just run into me in the grocery store. We hadn't seen him since he'd visited us over Christmas in 2001. A whiff of his stale breath when he spoke sent waves of nausea through me.

"Brian," I asked, shaking my head and closing the door, "what are you doing here at this hour?" I opened the door wider and let him step inside to the vestibule.

"I just drove to see Coach Collins earlier at the high school. Then I hung out with Justin." He paused. "Mom, I need a place to stay tonight."

"You drove three hours from Connecticut at this hour?"

"What's wrong with that?" he answered, with an edgy tone.

"You're not staying, Brian," Wayne said. He was standing behind me the entire time. I felt a mixture of relief that Wayne had taken charge and dread that I would have to send my son back out into the night. But I knew Wayne was right, and I vowed to stay strong in the face of the grim reality. I had to stop enabling my son.

Brian bristled in response and fixed his angry glare on me.

Walking over to the couch, I sat down and leaned forward. *Wayne was right not to let him stay because he had been drinking, but how could I turn my only son back out into that snowy night without a place to stay?*

Rocking back and forth in silence, I watched how Brian shifted his position and stared off into space as he stood in the entry.

Brian, stalling for time, said, "Can I see Muffin?"

Muffin, our long-haired yellow cat we adopted before we left Missouri in 1990, Brian's favorite, came around the corner. Brian lifted him close to his face, nuzzling him and rubbing his scruff. After a few minutes, he put him down and stood in silence.

I sat on the couch praying that I would find the words to say and the strength to get through the agonizing choice I had to make. My stomach wrenched with anxiety. A battle was raging in my head. *If I let him stay, will he ever leave and get better? He has to go, but how am I going to let him walk out into the snowy night?* I thought of his many relapses, his brushes with death, and his subsequent recoveries. At that moment, I realized I had no choice but to let him go. I had finally learned that my enabling behaviors were not helping him. Wayne stepped into the background and waited for my response.

After a few endless moments, I walked over to him. Taking a deep breath, choking back fear, I put my arms around his waist and said, "If anyone knows how to get help,

B, you do. I love you very much. Now go do what you know you need to do."

He looked at me with a blank stare, turned, walked out the door, got into his car, and disappeared into the snowy night. With my hands clenched into fists, I stood frozen in place and wondered if I would ever see him alive again.

It was my darkest moment—my only choice and his only chance. I would have to rely on my Higher Power—my God—to see us through.

CHAPTER 22

The Long, Winding Road to Recovery, 2002

Several months after sending Brian out into that snowy night in March of 2002, I learned through his sporadic phone calls to me that he'd found his way to another halfway house in Connecticut. By this time, I had lost count of the number of detox and rehab programs he'd attended. I had been told this about addiction—recovery often takes many attempts. I found consolation in the fact that he usually found his way into a program, but the sound of the phone ringing usually sent shivers down my spine. After a few of those phone calls, I started making the sign of the cross each time I picked up the phone. I wanted to hear from him to know he was still alive, all the while dreading that it was him. In May of 2002, he called after several months of no communication. I hadn't seen him since that March night.

"Hi, Mom," Brian said, his voice distant and hollow sounding.

"Hi, B. How are you?" I grimaced as I waited to hear the reason for his call.

"I'm in a homeless shelter near Danbury." As far as I knew, this was his first time in a homeless shelter.

Silence.

"Can you wire me some money for a one-way bus ticket home? I'll even check out programs in the area."

I bit my lip and held my head in my hand as I pondered my response. After a few seconds, I said,

"You can't live here, Brian. You need to find a way to get back into treatment."

"That means I have to get drunk so I can get into detox."

"Brian, if anyone knows the ropes, it's you."

I hung up the phone, hoping and praying I was doing the right thing. Messages from Al-Anon rang in my ears: "Do not do for your loved one what he can do for himself." I hated it that, each time I was confronted with a challenge related to Brian, I had to keep my son at a distance in order to find any kind of peace.

Within two weeks of his last phone call, I received a phone call from an alcohol counselor at McDonough House, a rehab facility outside of Danbury, Connecticut. Dr. Gill, the psychologist whom Brian had been seeing from Hartford, had arranged for Brian's admission, but he had to make it there on his own by bus. I had spoken with the counselor at the McDonough House while he was awaiting Brian's arrival. It terrified me that he had to get himself there by himself.

"He made it," the counselor said in a brief phone call.

"Thank God," I said, making the sign of the cross across my chest and slumping down in my chair in a moment of relief.

He stayed for one month, and, just as with his previous admissions to recovery programs, I was able to visit him after he was there two weeks. As I drove from New York through the rolling hills of southern Connecticut and saw the modest building at the top of a hill, surrounded by towering pine trees, I once again felt grateful that he was safe for the time being. I could only hope that he was learning and growing in healthy ways—ways that would help him get sober and move on in his life. But the hardest part of rehab for me was when he was discharged a month later. Being that this was his fourth rehabilitation program, I couldn't help but wonder how many more Brian would have to go through until he would be on the official road to recovery, if there even was such a thing.

As was his pattern after rehab, he continued to drink and wander around Connecticut. Most of the time, I had no idea of his whereabouts, which filled me with angst and fear. Around this time in 2003, I was working forty miles away, teaching nursing students at a community college in Albany and feeling well after the stem-cell transplant. The hour-long drive into work from Burnt Hills along the New York State Thruway left plenty of time to reflect and ponder Brian's most recent path following our phone call after he was discharged from the McDonough House. The deep pain of losing my son to alcohol lingered with my hopes as I stared straight ahead.

One morning during a time when I did not know Brian's whereabouts, I noticed a small clearing in the sky filled with dark, gray clouds. I prayed to know that Brian was alright. I wanted the clearing to be a rainbow, my ultimate symbol of hope, but all I saw was a bright ray shooting from behind the clouds, like a flashlight in the dark. I claimed it as validation that there would be better days ahead. When I returned from work around six o'clock that evening, the phone was ringing as I walked into the house.

"Hi, Mom," Brian said. It was an answer to a prayer. He was alive, and it felt good to hear his voice over the phone after all these weeks.

"Hey, B. I'm so happy to hear from you." It had been several months since we had last talked.

I cherished the moments when he was back, staying in touch with me.

"I'm in a halfway house in New Haven, Connecticut. It's near Yale."

"I knew you'd find your way, B," I said, smiling.

"It's a long-term one this time," he said.

I breathed a sigh of relief that he was back in treatment in a structured setting, where he would be attending meetings and meeting regularly with a counselor.

"Good—I'm so glad to hear this," I said.

I remembered that high school freshman son of mine who told his classmate he was going to win the Red Bat Award at the end of his baseball season for the highest batting average of the season. I had missed that feeling of optimism when Brian was in his element, doing the things he had always loved, making me feel he was always meant to be happy. I was sitting with one of his school friends at a picnic table at a gathering of Brian's friends in Cobyville, when he was fifteen, back in 1990.

"I'm not kidding you," Courtney said. "Brian told me that at the beginning of the season."

Just a few feet away, Brian was sparring with his buddies in the nearby stream, doing what fifteen-year-old boys should be doing—enjoying their friends. He walked on both sides of the fence between his good friends and his drug-using ones. It was a good day. He was with his good friends.

And he did win that award at the Spring assembly.

As I hung up the phone that day with a huge sigh of relief when Brian called for the first time in a long time, I felt the same hope for my son that I felt when Brian was fifteen. That twenty-seven-year-old son could do anything he set his mind to do. Even conquer his addiction.

I claimed it as a symbol of hope, just as I'd claimed the clearing in the sky that morning.

During this period of remission from cancer, I stayed on the lookout for new symptoms, since I was expected to follow up with my oncologist every six months. In the six years since cancer had invaded my body in 1996, I vowed to stay open to gratitude, considering how well I responded to chemotherapy and that it saved my life. But being grateful for my health also brought with it an ongoing need to catastrophize. A slight cough or cold, and suddenly I'd catch myself wondering if the cancer was back. Like a detective in search of a crime, I fervently examined the minute details in both my life and Brian's.

As it turned out, two years of chemotherapy had damaged my heart, requiring extensive follow-up with a cardiologist and treatment for congestive heart failure. That reality check was only the beginning. Six months later, in 1998, when I experienced my first episode of congestive heart failure, including shortness of breath, cough, and fatigue, it became clearer that I had been manipulating myself to avoid taking action. It was much more comfortable to be the one in charge rather than have to juggle integrating my roles as nurse and patient.

At the time, the stubborn nurse in me convinced my cardiologist to listen to my plea and take me off lifelong medications as long as I came for follow-up visits. As I left the exam room that day, he said,

"Come back to me when you have your first heart attack at ninety."

Despite my resistance to depending on medications, I changed cardiologists soon after.

Six months later, in 1998, I experienced another bout of congestive heart failure—shortness of breath, cough, fatigue. Second reality check.

"I have good news," I said to my friend Mary Sue when I phoned her from my hospital bed.

"The cancer didn't come back," I said, "but now I have congestive heart failure."

With that health scare, I adjusted my attitude and took the multiple medications without any resistance. Congestive heart failure is far more treatable than a cancer recurrence would be.

The doctor was wrong to let me stop the medications, and, with my nursing background, I should have known better. I began to understand firsthand how a patient's non-acceptance of a diagnosis can sabotage treatment and recovery. *But I thought I already knew that.* Even though the cancer was in remission, the repercussions of the chemotherapy kept me in a chronic-illness mode—on multiple medications and sitting in doctors' offices every three months.

I would soon begin to understand that my road to recovery would be long and winding. I'd have to learn to give up not knowing the outcomes related to my health. I didn't know where it was all leading or how to find any other way, so I kept walking, one day at a time. The message to my healing was all in the mess that I couldn't quite see. As long as I could be available to my children, that was all that mattered. Even though they were adults, I still felt the need to be there for them.

CHAPTER 23

Grant Street Rehab, 2002

In May 2002, the phone rang one evening,

"Hey, Mom. I just signed myself into Grant Street rehab in New Haven," Brian said.

"Good to hear, B. I've been worried since I haven't heard from you in three weeks," I said, breathing a heavy sigh of relief to hear his voice.

While at Grant Street working on his recovery, he was all excited about his next step, while I was still reeling from the insanity of his three-week binge into oblivion before his admission—the reign of terror and tears for me. I could still hear his voice: "Yeah, it got pretty bad. I was wandering around homeless, got blisters on my feet so bad I had to go to the ER, and I slept in an alley in the freezing rain one night."

After six months at the Grant Street rehabilitation center, I mustered the courage to visit him, not quite sure how his release would affect us both. He was scheduled for discharge within the next few months, and I wanted to grab the rare opportunity to see him on his birthday, curious and eager to know how he had changed, if at all.

It was a sunny, crisp October day in 2002 when I drove up to the stark, brick building in a rundown neighborhood in New Haven, Connecticut. I thought about all the choices that had led my son and me to this place. *Will he pull it off this time?* Of the many rehab programs he'd attended in the past, this was the longest program he had committed to. Of course, I was hopeful he would begin to take responsibility for his life and be able to move on in a healthy way, but I also knew that it would take a monumental effort on both our parts to help him overcome addiction.

As soon as I parked the car on the street and got out, Brian came running to me with open arms. His thick hair, overdue for a cut, was the first thing I noticed. I was happy to see him.

"Hey, Mom. Great to see you," he said as we hugged and he twirled me around. "How long has it been?"

"I can't remember for sure, but I think it was last October during your first semester at Bridgeport. It's been way too long." I quickly went through the previous months in my head. *Had it been an entire year since we'd seen each other?* Overall, one year's absence isn't uncommon in the world of recovery and addiction, and yet all those sleepless nights of worry and anxiety had consumed me and affected my own healing.

"Wow, a whole year ago," he said.

"Well, we're together now, and that's what counts," I said, soaking up the moment.

"Happy Birthday!"

We walked into the building and sat in the community room as he recounted what had led him there and how it was going.

"Look at me, Mom. Twenty-seven years old and hanging out with a bunch of burn-outs. What's wrong with me?" he said.

"Only you can answer that one, B," I said, looking around at the dingy white walls and watching wrinkled, weary men of all ages meander around.

My son's own rumpled look, with baggy jeans and an oversized plaid flannel shirt, saddened me.

"Mom, when I got here, I had only the clothes on my back, and they were pretty raunchy. People donate clothes, and I picked through a bin to find some that fit."

I recalled the times when, as a teenager, he would spend endless moments preening in front of the mirror, rubbing his hair and viewing himself from different angles, a stunning contrast to the young man sitting in front of me.

We left the facility, and I took him shopping for some clothes and shoes. We drove to the Yale campus and walked around. Then we had a delicious dinner at an Italian restaurant near the campus.

"Mom," he said, after we ordered, "sometimes I wonder why I was born. I mean, you don't deserve to have to put up with all I've put you through."

"Brian," I said, my heart stuck in my throat, "you are a special gift from God. God knew exactly what He was doing when he made me your mother." I reached my hands across the table, and he held them. Tears welled up in our eyes. It was heartwarming to have Brian acknowledge the hell he had put me through—treatment I didn't deserve yet seemed to tolerate far beyond what would be expected. The guilt and shame of not providing a stable home—two divorces and frequent moves—still bubbled under the surface and drove my actions. Still, in this moment, my heart was full.

After dinner, we walked around the downtown section, drifting into and out of stores.

I tried to enjoy the moments of being with Brian. While an uncertain future loomed before us, I remained steadfast in my hope that Brian would someday recover. That meant letting go of my need to control his actions. He would have to do the work. But I also knew I had to do my own work on myself.

The next morning, I picked him up at Grant Street, and we went to Mass on campus and then out for breakfast. While at Mass, I noticed an attractive young woman staring at Brian, my tall, handsome son with the big, dark eyes and ready smile. For that moment, I imagined him living a sober life and finding a loving mate. *Dear God, help Brian see his goodness and awaken to the precious life you have given him.*

We went to breakfast after Mass. I looked across the table into his eyes, and I knew in my heart he was still struggling—shifting eyes, downward glances, dull stares back at me.

I looked at him with eyebrows raised.

"Mom, I'll be fine," he said.

I handed him a handwritten letter I'd taken the time to write after last evening's dinner. As a writer, I was called to express the pain I was feeling about getting my son back. Ironically, his recovery triggered my own fear that I'd lose him once again to alcohol. As a last resort, I buckled down with my words to guide him "home"—words meant to nurture hope for myself as much as for him.

As I handed him the letter, I thought back to the many times I'd had to navigate my own fears and insecurities, not quite sure if I had what it takes to fully understand the work it would take to truly be emotionally present for Brian. There is a saying by Hippocrates that "Healing is a matter of time, but it is sometimes a matter of opportunity."

My Dear Son,

You asked me last night why God gave me you. You are a blessing to me, Brian. I wish you could see in yourself what I see in you. I know you are struggling, but hear me out . . .

When you were an infant, I remember looking at you and feeling so blessed that you were a special gift from God and that God had special plans for you. Honestly! Well, I still feel that way. I believe our greatest obstacles can be our greatest blessings. We can become stronger and learn lessons which we couldn't learn in any other way. God also gives us a free will, and we all make choices—some good, some not so good. But each "failure" is an opportunity to learn, become stronger, and do better the next time.

You are here for a reason, Brian. I don't know what your future holds, but I do know you have a lot of ingredients for success. The question is: How badly do you want to change and do what it takes to turn your life around? I really believe you need to think about that and answer that question for yourself.

You are hanging onto the past and allowing yourself to wallow in this rut of negative thinking and self-defeating attitudes.

Is this where you want to stay? You are the only one who can decide to get yourself out of this rut. And sometimes, we have to "fake it till we make it."

It's time to take action, put one foot in front of the other—get a job, start paying your bills, continue treatment—one day, one hour, one minute at a time. You don't have to like it. Just do it!

We all have to take care of our own needs, but there comes a time when we need to reach beyond ourselves and put our focus on other people and responsibilities. And I don't mean neglecting ourselves. It seems to me you have too much time to be self-absorbed and obsessed with your faults and failures.

How about switching that "stinkin' thinkin'" to your assets—your health, your youth, your early recovery, your opportunity through the halfway house and VA Program to get your life back in order. Your incredible God-given talents and abilities. Your time in the Air Force was a gift to let you know what you are capable of. They're there, those same talents and skills. You just have to work at getting them back.

Look around, B. You will always find someone else worse off than you. I'm not encouraging you to compare yourself with others, but we all have something we're struggling with. You are not alone or that terribly unique.

Give yourself the rest of the day to wallow. Then wake up tomorrow determined (even if you have to fake it) to take action. I suggest you use the VA resources to discuss your debts. Maybe they can help you figure out a way to resolve it.

"The journey of a thousand miles starts with one step." You've been given another chance. I remain very hopeful. I know you can do it. Like I said earlier, the question you have to answer is: Do you want to make the necessary changes?

"Trust in God, and keep rowing to shore."

My love and prayers are always with you,
Mom

I needed to heed my own words for myself and my healing as much as I felt Brian needed them for his healing. Part of my healing would mean forgiving myself for not providing my children with a father and a stable home life.

CHAPTER 24

Christmas of Hope, 2002

2002 was one of those sad years, with Brian's admission to Grant Street. It was not yet clear if the rehabilitation program was working for him, if he was serious about his own recovery. The Christmas of 2002, after my visit to Grant Street, was especially hard since I knew Brian wouldn't be coming home for the holidays.

I hadn't seen him since my October visit to Grant Street Partnership, but a phone call from Brian two weeks before Christmas was just the thing I needed to lift my spirits. My body throbbed with fear and uneasiness . . . a sad contrast to Burl Ives' *Holly, Jolly Christmas* tune blaring from the stereo . . . I said "goodbye" to Brian at the long-term alcohol rehabilitation program he'd signed himself into in July. He had just turned twenty-seven.

When Brian had phoned me a few weeks before Christmas, he cheerfully told me his plans. Rather than following staff recommendations to live in a halfway house, he planned to take a bus to New York City to pursue his dream of acting.

"I want to get back into acting, Mom," he said.

I recalled the rave reviews he'd received when he played Biff in *Death of a Salesman* when he was stationed in Fairbanks, Alaska, while in the Air Force. In the scene where he had to cry, he made himself think about the night his father passed out in my doorway before we were married; for his character's part, it made him sob uncontrollably, leaving the audience stunned. I knew he had the passion and heart for acting, yet I wondered how he could just take off, and I worried about his safety. But the halfway house was voluntary, and his commitment to it was a condition for admission.

"Mom, I've always wanted to get back into acting. This is my chance," he said.

"But where will you live?" I asked, feeling panic setting in. "What about a halfway house for a while?" I added.

"I'm done, Mom. How many halfway houses can I live in? It's time for me to strike out on my own."

I knew no amount of my advice would carry any weight. I also had a new set of worries—my fresh-out-of-rehab son wandering aimlessly in the world's biggest city. He had never even been there.

Though I felt distraught about Brian, knowing he wouldn't be joining us for Christmas, I still hung on to many hopes and dreams for Brian. What mother doesn't dream and hope for her son?

Each year when I put the cross ornament on the tree, I am reminded how Christmas can be a symbol of hope. As I looked at the cross, it reminded "me" of the power of the cross—a cross I bore as I prayed for my son's life. I thought of the cross that Jesus died on so that I might have eternal life and salvation. I believed. Looking at the cross renewed my hope in Brian's recovery, and I put my trust in my faith that all would be well.

Every year when I prepared to decorate our Christmas tree, I hauled out the large blue plastic bins and unwrapped all the ornaments, laying them out on the couch. Each one conjured up a specific memory of Christmases past—some happy, some sad.

There was the plastic Christmas angel for the top of the tree from my paternal grandmother, Lydia, the Mr. and Mrs Santa from my maternal grandmother, Nan, the green John Deere tractor, the white dove from my dear friend Judy. As I pulled out the ornaments and examined each one, they took me to warm memories of family and friendship, with my thoughts turning to Brian and wondering where he would be at Christmas.

I stared at a ragged green star ornament I was holding in my hands. In the center was a photo of Brian as a six-week-old baby—a hand-crafted gift from his preschool years.

Such a beautiful baby boy.

His red-checkered outfit with a white collar hugged his chubby little boy's body. I lingered for a moment before I hung the green star-shaped ornament . . . the points frayed and bent from the years of life and Christmases past. I melted into his soft, dark eyes.

Then I found it—the Hallmark cross with the word "hope" inscribed in the middle beneath a plastic dome. It was a gift I had bought for myself during another sad time in 2000, when Brian was in the throes of his addiction, wandering aimlessly around Connecticut.

I knew there would always be difficult days, but this Christmas felt unusually difficult. When your adult child is an alcoholic, the letting-go process becomes even harder. It scared me witless to imagine him alone in New York City without a job or a support system.

The gold-and-white cross dangled near the top of the Christmas tree . . . with "Hope" emblazoned in the center beneath a clear plastic dome . . . a gift to myself, a tangible sign of hope. I stood back after hanging it on the Fraser fir bough. The tree's pungent odor was reminiscent of Christmases past, when my children were young.

I stood back, admiring the cross, contemplating it from every angle. The center of the cross reflected the lights of the tree. On branches beneath the cross, gold and red ornaments glistened with the words "faith" and "joy." I wanted to be reminded of the feelings of hope every time I caught sight of the light of the sparkling cross when I walked into the room.

But this Christmas season was now upon me. My faith in God gave me the strength to hope for his recovery . . . to believe that, one day, he and I would hang that cross ornament on the tree together.

I sat on the couch and wrote myself a note to enclose in the ornament box: "This ornament is a reminder to remain ever faithful and hopeful in Brian's recovery."

I turned off the tree lights.

One day at a time. . . .

I prayed for the strength to endure.

Hope matters, and life goes on to give us moments of joy in the midst of our sad moments.

But to nurture this hope, I knew I needed to do something tangible for myself to try to fill the deep hole in my soul. Despite grieving over the absence of my son, it gave me joy to adopt a poor family affected by alcohol abuse—a mother, grandmother, and three school-aged children—through the Bethesda House, an interfaith ministry to the homeless and disabled in our community, and give them a Christmas.

"No gifts for me this year. I want each of you to pick a name and buy a gift for a family member in honor of Brian's sobriety," I told our five children. It was a change in tradition, but all of them got caught up in the excitement of helping a poor family in Brian's name.

By Christmas, the wrapped gifts under our tree extended halfway into the living room. I added in boxes of extra nonperishable food sitting in our garage from Brian's vacated Connecticut apartment.

Since I had to work, Wayne delivered the load to the Bethesda House, five days before Christmas.

"It was almost embarrassing," he said, returning empty-handed. "All the packages took up several tables."

My only regret was that the Bethesda House stipulated that the donation had to be anonymous, and I would not get a chance to meet this family and watch them opening their gifts. However, the thought that they were given in honor of Brian's sobriety consoled me.

Giving this family a Christmas in Brian's name sustained my hope for his future sobriety despite his absence. I did it for me as much as I did it for them.

CHAPTER 25

Waiting for the Prodigal Son, 2003

"French toast and strawberries," I told the waitress at the diner.

Wayne and I were enjoying a beautiful Cape Cod October morning celebrating our second wedding anniversary in October 2003. Ten months had passed since Brian's impulsive decision to go to New York City during Christmastime.

While waiting for the order, I was drawn to a painting on the wall of three empty rocking chairs on a country porch, envisioning a scene where Brian would finally return home again. I stared at the picture as if to soak up the hope it represented as a way of comforting myself. We were in one of those non-communication periods with Brian. Phone calls over the past year since visiting him at Grant Street the previous October were sporadic and unpredictable, making it clear that he was not in recovery. Each day tested my ability to stay mentally and emotionally focused without worrying about his whereabouts.

"Where are you, Kathy?" Wayne said, leaning forward in his seat. His concerned gaze brought me back to the moment.

"That feeling never seems to go away," I said, still looking at the painting. "I mean, the feeling that my son is going to die if he doesn't stop drinking."

"How so?" he asked, quietly, leaning forward, listening.

"I can just see the drinking taking over his life. My sensitive young man with so much promise and potential has repeatedly traded his talents for the lure of the bottle."

I stared at the painting again. This time, my eyes welled up with tears.

"I know I have no control over Brian's choices, but I know I can continue to pray," I said, looking at Wayne, who nodded in agreement. Wayne's quiet, supportive presence calmed my despair.

I was searching for my own words of comfort as I sat with the realization that the hope I clung to had been tempered by the stark and painful realization that Brian's addiction was progressing—he was drinking more and isolating himself. Though I never saw Brian drinking, I witnessed the aftermath—slurred speech, glassy eyes, stumbling gait. This was not what I had envisioned when I took him out for his birthday. As far as I could surmise by his occasional garbled phone calls at all hours, he drank excessively and created havoc, in essence, sabotaging any chance to succeed by jeopardizing his means of taking care of himself.

After finishing breakfast, we walked to the nearby beach, finding comfort in the simple presence of each other. We walked along the white sandy shoreline, watching the sandpipers scurry about and listening to the hollow sound of the waves lapping against the shore.

With each step on the beach, I visualized Brian recovering and inviting Wayne and me to an AA meeting where he gave his testimony. I took another step toward harnessing positive energy by visualizing him healthy and strong. I visualized the sweet, loving little boy known mostly for his dancing eyes, infectious smile, and caring spirit growing into a healthy, sober man. *Please, God, watch over him. Keep him safe.*

I stopped along the shore and picked up a large, pearly gray shell. Then, I wrote the word "fear" in big letters in the moist sand. As I watched the tide wash the word "fear" away, I mustered the courage to believe that Brian and I could be healed.

Watching each letter wash away reminded me of how I'd pined for hope, waiting to hear from Brian.

During the times of waiting for Brian, I'd attended a women's retreat centered around the theme of "Hope" in February 2003 at a local Dominican retreat center. The retreat leader, Father Deimke, reminded me about the importance of renewing hope—"what the Lord has in store. It could be wonderful," he said.

Father Deimke's words inspired me to keep on hoping, despite the dire circumstances. Staying in fear is a choice. Feeling afraid is just that—a feeling. I couldn't change the circumstances, but I could choose not to give in to the despair and begin to trust. Perhaps this is why I felt compelled to write the word "fear" in the sand that October day eight months later. It was a starting point toward opening myself up to trust. And if I could trust myself and my Higher Power, I could also trust that Brian would find his way home.

Looking out over the great expanse, the ocean sparkled and went on forever, like the love I had for my son and the hope that he would someday recover.

CHAPTER 26

Hope Amid Faces of Horror, 2004

"Cancer unit."

I felt a sharp jolt go through my body.

The chair of the nursing department at Maria College, where I taught nursing students who needed clinical exposure in a hospital setting, had just given me my clinical assignment for the spring semester. Teaching in an amphitheater filled with sixty eager adult students ranging in age from eighteen to fifty seemed like a cinch compared to supervising students in the clinical area. Though I valued staying up to date with the latest standards of care, I loved being at the patient's bedside and guiding students in the direct care of patients.

"It's a challenging hospital unit, Kathy," she said, "and I need a strong person in that role."

I nodded in response and said, "I appreciate your confidence in me." But I felt shaky inside.

The cancer unit in the local tertiary medical center in Albany, New York, caring for the region's sickest patients, also admitted overflow patients with medical-surgical needs. I felt an immediate shudder.

It had been about six years since my last hospitalization for Non-Hodgkin's Lymphoma. Time enough to heal. *So why do I feel like crying? Why can't I catch my breath?* By then, I had left her office, on the verge of tears, and needed to talk with Wayne. I rushed down the hall, closed my office door, and sat down to dial Wayne at home.

"Wayne," I sobbed into the phone. "I don't think I can do it." The tears wouldn't stop. Clearly, a fear had been triggered. Death was an ever-present reality for both Brian and me. As much as I tried not to focus on this, this current assignment stirred up memories of facing my mortality as a cancer patient.

"Of course, you can. Maybe this will make you stronger," he said in his characteristic, level-headed way.

To my surprise, although I felt some reluctance toward caring for cancer patients, I made a conscious decision to face my discomfort and work through it. Determined to give the students the best possible experience, I forced myself to deal directly with a dying cancer patient and found the courage to face my fears. I had survived cancer, and I would focus on my strengths, not my weaknesses, as hard as I knew that would be. The image of the tide washing away the word "fear" during our recent trip to Cape Cod reminded me to trust. Yet, I still hadn't reconciled my fears.

By the time I arrived home, an hour later, I decided to view my assignment as a way to face my fears of reliving my own cancer experience through my patients.

Once again, Wayne's steadfast support and cool logic had inspired me. One of my first patients I assigned to a student a few days later during this clinical rotation was Pamela, a thirty-seven-year-old woman with end-stage cancer of the appendix. Looking down at her lying in the hospital bed, her gaunt expression and sunken eyes signaling impending death, I felt the horror of my initial diagnosis and immense gratitude for my second chance. A young life cut short represented the fine line that divided us.

When I returned home that night, my tears of gratitude that my life had been spared spilled over into my sadness for another life devastated by the ravages of cancer. I knew I would have a reaction and gave myself permission to face the feelings and work through them as they came up. The driving force behind this was my desire to offer the students a rich experience. I reminded myself that I had survived cancer and had the strength to face this fear. I needed to muster all the courage I could to face this setback as well as face the ongoing uncertainty about Brian.

It was only three days later when I met an alcoholic patient named Bill with late-stage cirrhosis. I knew by the queasy feeling in my stomach that I was out of my comfort zone and into Brian's world, which always left me feeling uneasy. As far as I knew, Brian was still homeless in New York City after leaving a long-term rehab in Connecticut right before Christmas. He had chosen to pursue an acting career rather than go into a halfway house. From that moment, I felt he was doomed from the start.

I braced myself as I walked into Bill's hospital room with my student, a fifty-year-old operating-room nurse at the hospital, married with two adult children, ages twenty and twenty-three. Bill had been admitted to the unit a week ago. His yellow skin and eyeballs and distended abdomen (ascites) from the fluid left no doubt that he had end-stage cirrhosis. *Please, God, let Brian wake up before he reaches this point.*

I wanted to take Bill's picture to send to Brian as a wake-up call. The reality that Brian could become this patient someday haunted me. I was looking at what Brian could become if he continued drinking. The pain of waiting out his visits and calls, only to be left hanging concerning his whereabouts clued me into my biggest fear—his possible encounter with death. *What will become of him? When will he wake up and take responsibility for his life? Will he wake up?*

Haunted by Bill's image, I immediately wrote Brian a letter that night to describe what I saw every time I taught this group of students, hoping he would get this letter at the homeless shelter.

Each time the student and I walked into his room during the four-week rotation, Bill greeted us like we were long-lost friends.

"Hey, come on in," Bill motioned with a smile one day. "What can I teach you today?"

He reminded me of Brian and how good he was at covering up his pain with his smile and gift for small talk.

At first glance, Bill seemed vibrant and sociable. Bigger than life, his 6'4" frame consumed the bed. I imagined him in his better days, lighting up the operating room with his personality and banter, like Brian could light up a room with his charm and wit. The mask of congeniality was familiar. As a result of his chronic liver failure, Bill had kidney failure requiring dialysis and a lower-leg infection with a tunnel from his achilles tendon to his knee. The ascites (fluid) made him look like he was nine months pregnant as he struggled to breathe and move in the bed. The student had to pack his leg wound with a dressing under my supervision. As I guided the student in the procedure, Bill chimed in with his own advice about the procedure.

"Take the forceps and gently guide the gauze into the hole," he said to the student, pointing and nodding his approval as she began packing the wound.

His need to hang on to some control over his life was part of the care plan the student and I had discussed, so she was prepared in advance for his involvement in the dressing change.

"My last drink was six months ago, but my liver is so far gone from years of drinking that my prognosis is poor." As the student continued dressing his wound, Bill chatted as if he were describing a change in vacation plans.

The most we could do was to try to make him comfortable. Death would be painful and messy. Judging by his symptoms, it would also be rapid, probably a matter of weeks. These patients often bleed to death when the distended blood vessels in their esophagus, caused by backed-up pressure from the damaged liver, ruptured. *Please, God. Let Brian wake up in time.*

The nurse in me kept Bill at an emotional distance, but the mother in me screamed out in silent grief for my son.

Please, God. Let Brian wake up in time.

Like Bill, Brian could stop this process by not drinking. It can be reversed and controlled by sobriety and abstinence alone. But after a certain point, the physical damage becomes irreversible. Although I had feared for his life ever since he'd started drinking thirteen years ago, I felt an urgency to write and tell him in graphic detail what alcohol can do to the body. His clock was ticking. My frantic mind would not rest. The frustrating part about addiction is that, until the person decides to stop using their drug of choice, there is little one can do, other than to keep loving them and supporting them in their attempts at sobriety.

Paralyzed with fear for Brian's life, in the letter to Brian I wrote later that night, I detailed Bill's case. I wrote everything from what alcohol could do to the body to my plea to get him to see that there was an irreversible link between drinking and death. I ended the letter with this:

> *AA says, "Alcoholism is a disease of terminal uniqueness." Nobody thinks it will happen to them; nobody thinks s/he will one day lie in a hospital bed, writhing in agony from delirium tremens (DTs) or having a belly as big as a nine-month pregnant uterus . . .*
>
> *So controllable and reversible . . . if only Bill had made the decision to fight for recovery in his 20s.*
>
> *With Faith, Hope, and Love,*
> *Mom*

Unknown to me at the time, a year later, Leigh Ann confessed to me that she, too, wrote her brother a letter telling him how much she missed him—recalling childhood memories—begging him to get help "before it's too late."

We both hoped our letters would make it to the homeless shelter where we thought he was staying. I felt reassured when the letters were not returned to sender. I could only hope, wait, and pray.

CHAPTER 27

New York City Dreaming, 2004

The image of Bill haunted me for months after I finished my clinical rotation with the students in the spring of 2004. The rotation ended before Bill died, and I lost track of him after we left. I could only imagine the painful death he endured. I got caught up in the fear of Brian following in the same path. It usually took about three weeks before I started getting shaky and nervous about Brian if I hadn't heard from him. I had to force myself not to give in to negative thoughts about his whereabouts. Prayer and Al-Anon meetings were my lifelines over the next six months following my clinical rotation. My mantra became, "My faith is greater than my fear."

But when he did call, his sporadic, frantic phone calls at odd hours fueled my anxiety into overdrive. I entertained not answering the phone, but I knew it was him, and, desperately needing to hear his voice, I picked up the phone each time. I had not seen him since October 2002, nearly eighteen months before, when I hugged him goodbye in front of Grant Street on his birthday weekend. It was clear to me then that I needed help as much as he did, and back to Al-Anon I went. I needed to take care of myself whether he got better or not.

On his twenty-eighth birthday in October of 2003, he had called me every two hours, starting at six in the morning, and right away, I knew something was up, given that he had not been communicating with me for the past eighteen months. Brian had worked as a street vendor since first arriving in the city in 2002.

As it turned out, while Brian was in New York City, he signed himself into an alcohol-detox unit that night, only to sign himself out forty-eight hours later. It seemed to me that he often called when he had been to detox and rehab and he needed something. At some point, he told me that he'd moved from the homeless shelter to a rented room.

"I'm broke and hungry," he said, breathless and fast-paced. "I just signed myself out of detox. My room is a mess. I lost my vendor's license."

His litany played on and on, but all I could do was listen. The question that plagued me was: How was I, a mother, ever going to be able to move on in my life while my son kept dancing with the devil? It seemed to me there were three of us in this dance.

"I love you, B," I said, ending the conversation. "Happy Birthday."

Over the next few months, he called a few times, and we had brief conversations. I always wanted to know how he was doing, and I eagerly awaited the news that he was taking some personal responsibility.

"Not much new, Mom. I'm still renting a room."

The following year and a few months after I had sent him the letter about Bill, on May 6, 2004, he sent me a letter inside a Mother's Day card that read:

Mom,

I hope you have a special Mother's Day. You certainly deserve a day devoted to you.

I have some news since we last spoke—whether good or bad is to be determined. I moved into the place I was telling you about. I had about 10 days to make the decision, and I chose to go for it. I felt I needed to get away from the situation I was living in. Especially from the mental health aspect. I'll finally have some peace and serenity I haven't experienced in quite a while.

The bad days still seem to be outweighing the good, but I suppose ultimately I'm the one in control of that. That's much easier said than done. I feel very distant from where I want to be. I get stuck in my own head, and there are times when that's the worst place to be.

Regardless, I must forge on day by day and only hope God's plan begins to show life, even minutely. I pray he helps me overcome my fears and fills me with the strength and confidence I once had. I pray for healthy friends to steer me toward the good and away from the bad. I pray for a set of values, however simple, to base my life on, on a daily basis. I pray the Lord to bring me a new vision, a consistent vision in which I do not have to look back. I pray he brings me back to my beautiful family.

I think that'll do it for now. Well, I didn't plan on it, but I just prayed on paper—now it's etched in stone.

Mom, I hope you have a great day. I love you and think of you often.

Brian

"Prayed on paper." My son knows God! I stared at the words, and my heart filled with joy and relief. The son I always knew was there gave me a glimpse of normalcy, a kernel of hope to get me through another day. It was not the first time he'd sent me a heartfelt letter. Although it was rare, I cherished every word. For the remainder of 2004, I heard from him sporadically, and, during the times I didn't hear from him, I pulled out this letter to remind myself that, underneath his disease, my son was healthy and whole. I let these thoughts buoy me. I learned to not to ask too many questions.

A few weeks later, on May 17, 2004, I had a dream about visiting Brian in New York and woke up feeling more hopeful than ever.

In the dream, I was standing in his new apartment, noting how things weren't nearly as bad as I imagined. Even though it looked a little messy, Brian looked and sounded well and had comfortable surroundings and caring, friendly neighbors.

I realized I'd left the younger Brian in the car as well as a big pot of pasta by the steering wheel.

"I want you to get acquainted with your younger self," I said to Brian as we stood in his new apartment.

As we rushed together to the car, the younger Brian had turned the heat down and removed the pot so it didn't boil over.

To me, this dream was a sign that Brian had begun to take responsibility as an adult. It also meant that I wanted the adult Brian to get in touch with that precious little boy who stole my heart all those years ago. I missed him so much, both the younger and older versions, and I wanted to see him as soon as possible. The dream made me feel it would be safe. It confirmed that the time to visit him in New York City was right. It had been twenty months since I had seen him.

After making arrangements with Brian, on June 12, 2004, Leigh Ann and I rode Amtrak from Troy-Rensselaer to Penn Station. Before we boarded the train, I had shared the dream with Leigh Ann, and she, too, agreed it was time. As the trees along the banks of the Hudson River flashed by, the memories of Brian flashed through my mind—the good times and not-so-good times. I chose to focus on making it a good day. I made it my intention to look Brian in the eye and hug him, pushing aside any worries about how he really was doing. During this time, I assumed he had the best intentions to do right with his life.

Leigh Ann and I were lost in our own thoughts during the ride, not speaking for the two-and-a-half-hour trip. She was single, working in her first teaching job and preparing for her summer job. I wondered how she was feeling, since her relationship with her brother was so tenuous due to the chaos his drinking had created in our family. I understood her reluctance to engage with her brother and chose not to question her. As desperately as I wanted them to bond as siblings—I always held out hope for that—I respected her need for time and space to figure out her relationship with him. I was happy she'd agreed to come.

As the train screeched to a stop at Penn Station, my heart raced. We climbed the stairs to the main level, and I hoped it wouldn't take too long to find Brian in the mass of people.

"There he is," Leigh Ann said, pointing ahead.

There he was, at the head of the staircase, tall, casually dressed, and handsome. *Oh, my God! He showed up!* Even though he had given me every indication on the phone that he was getting his life together, I had tried to set my expectations low, since I never knew with Brian. My first thought: *He must be sober, or he wouldn't have shown up.*

"Hey, guys," he said with arms outstretched, ready to hug us both.

After he hugged Leigh Ann, I fell into his big, sturdy arms, held on, and then stood back.

"You're looking great, B." I saw that his eyes were clear and bright, a sign to me that he was not drinking.

"Thanks, Mom. I'm doing OK."

"Show us your city, B."

We walked outside into a warm, sunny day with no particular place in mind. The sights and sounds of the city bombarded us as hordes of people scurried by. A sidewalk juggling act kept us occupied for a while. Suddenly we found ourselves at Central Park and decided to walk around and eat lunch at one of the cafés. There was so much to say, and, despite the fact that so much time had elapsed, we kept walking in relative silence, making small talk every so often. I soaked up the feeling of normalcy, reminding me of the times when I took my children to the park when they were babies.

Brian was relaxed as he directed us to a nearby restaurant in the park.

The three of us settled in at our patio table and looked over our menus. After getting our food, midway through, Brian broke the silence. Looking straight into our eyes, he said,

"Hey, guys. I read your letters to me."

Letters? The ones we had written to him in January? It was now June.

"Really?" I said, feeling flush with hope that our pleas had reached him.

"Yeah, I know what you are saying, and I appreciate you both writing me."

I looked over at Leigh Ann, who gave a faint smile.

"I found an apartment in Queens and moved in with a new roommate last month. He's a musician and a great guy. I wanted to wait to tell you, and when I knew you were coming, I decided this was the time to break it to you. You know I also started back working as a street vendor, selling jackets, sunglasses, and watches."

"That's great, B," I said, taking it all in as I inhaled deeply and then slowly released my stored-up tension. This was huge, since he had long periods of not working due to his drinking.

"Good news, B," Leigh Ann added, nodding her approval.

He was moving on in his life. As I soaked up the rest of the day, sharing these moments with both my adult kids, enjoying my son, and daring to hope in his future, I felt my dream had come true. I was under no illusion that all was well with Brian, but it was a start. I could begin to trust that Brian was capable of taking care of himself.

CHAPTER 28

Ebb and Flow, 2006

I don't remember the exact moment it happened, but, somewhere along the way, I felt stirrings inside that things were going to be different. Brian experienced several long periods of sobriety over the next two years when he excelled in his work as a vendor in New York City, began dating, and even traveled to Italy with one of his girlfriends. Though it was a relief, I also knew that I could count on only one day at a time. I had backed off questioning him. I began to get a sense of what life with a sober son felt like, though I never relaxed into that notion with any degree of confidence. Though he had achieved several previous periods of sobriety, this two-year time frame was the longest period. At thirty-one, he had returned, filling me with joy and relief.

During one of his sober periods in 2006, he visited our family cottage. It was my annual vacation. Wayne had stayed home to maintain his four-acre garden and go to the farmer's market. Brian brought his new girlfriend, Karen, a tall, attractive blonde with long, flowing curls and a wide smile. They took me out to dinner for my sixtieth birthday at a lovely lakeside restaurant with a deck overlooking the water. As I watched the seagulls on the shore and felt the gentle breezes off the lake, I cherished having my son back, looking and acting normal, for an extended period of time. The gratitude I felt for the blessings of remission from cancer and restoration of my health brimmed to capacity and added to my joy. But my anxiety about his ability to maintain sobriety lingered. When he started dating Karen, I wondered if she knew about his past. *Was he being honest with her?* From across the table, I watched them glancing at each other and smiling, her gleaming blue eyes focused on Brian as he spoke. She set my mind at ease before our dinner was served.

"I Googled his name when we first met and found out about him being picked up for marijuana possession in Bridgeport. When I asked him about his past, he told me the truth about his drinking problem."

"Yeah, I did, Mom." Brian nodded, "I'm ready to admit my mistakes and move on."

I took a cleansing breath and relaxed into the moment.

The waiter stopped by to take our orders.

"Order anything you want, Mom," Brian said. "The treat's on me." I relished the rare moment—my son taking me out to dinner.

For the next few days at the lake, I soaked up Brian's return as I watched him spar with his uncles, Tom and Gary, on the dock in good-natured shoving and pushing. And the image of him sitting on the beach swing, talking with Grandpa, warmed my heart. I was hopeful this time with family would strengthen him for his long-haul daily battle with addiction. I had longed for these moments, afraid that I would never witness them again. To stay hopeful for the long term, I continued to visualize them in daydreams. I prayed endlessly for the day to come when I could see my son for the capable, kindhearted young man I knew him to be beneath all the wreckage and manipulation of his alcohol use. I wanted these moments to last forever and to forget the terror of fearing for his life every time he drank. But I had no control over his choice to drink or not drink. I proceeded cautiously . . . *do I serve wine with dinner or lock it up?* His sobriety became new territory for both of us. It felt that way any time he'd achieved it in the past, and this was no different. Until he could achieve sobriety in the long term, these periods would be a challenge. But with each new period of sobriety, my hope for his long-term sobriety was strengthened. I treaded lightly, though, as I tried to focus on enjoying the moment without projecting too far into the future.

Several months later, in November of 2006, while working as a nurse practitioner in an urgent-care setting near my home, I received a phone call.

"Kathy, there's a Karen Clark on the phone for you," my co-worker Nancy announced, peeking her head into my office.

A sense of dread engulfed me as our eyes locked in silent understanding. My heart started pounding, and I felt a cold chill run through my body. Nancy knew my story about the impact of Brian's drinking on me. I walked to the nurses' station, saying a silent prayer all the way down the hall. *Dear Lord, give me strength. This can't be good.*

I reached for the phone in slow motion and sat down with a heaviness that reminded me of previous relapses. I had witnessed two years of Brian's sobriety, and I was fearful that my hard-earned confidence in my son and myself would now pull me asunder. I was holding out for his long-term recovery.

"Hello," I said, reluctantly and with trepidation.

"Brian started drinking, and I don't know where he is," Karen sobbed.

Laden with sorrow, I remained silent for a moment. My chest tightened.

"What happened?" I asked, not really wanting to hear this but knowing that there was no choice but to listen.

"I guess he's been drinking since Thanksgiving after being sober for the past two years, and I didn't know it. He's acting so weird, and I can't believe he's gone."

After a while, his relapses became routine to me over the course of the nineteen years of his drinking. Every relapse brought a fresh wave of terror that Karen couldn't possibly see or understand, and still, I went into counselor mode—it was the only way I could protect myself and help Karen.

"Karen, I know this must be very hard for you. Please hear me out. Brian is an alcoholic, and he needs to stop drinking. You can't make him do it." Even though he had divulged his past problems with drinking, it was hard for her to comprehend his current state.

"I'm so scared," she cried and then tried to catch her breath. "What if he dies?"

The Al-Anon slogan, "You didn't cause it, you can't control it, and you can't cure it" ran through my head.

"Karen, we didn't cause Brian to drink, nor can we control his decisions. You must learn to take care of yourself. Can you get to an Al-Anon meeting today?"

"Maybe, but I'm worried about him."

The haunting image of my patient Bill dying of cirrhosis came back to me.

"I am, too. All we can do at this point is pray and not support his drinking."

After our conversation, I braced myself for the predictable chaos that would ensue . . . frantic phone calls, attempts to manipulate, and long periods of uncertainty where I obsessed whether he was dead or alive. I was both helpless and fragile over this disease as I navigated the ropes of fear that gripped me each time I had to face his downward spirals. Hope was all I had.

Brian's drinking had essentially taken over for that week of the Christmas season of 2006, and I had to continue to embrace the one-day-at-a-time mindset. Several weeks went by with sporadic, frantic phone calls from Karen about Brian going into and out of emergency rooms and signing himself out of detox units. With each call, my hard-earned sense of hope plummeted a little further. At one point after about ten days, Brian went missing. Hopelessness threatened my sense of inner peace during my shift in the Urgent Care setting of the hospital. *Dear Lord, bring my hope back. That's all I want, for without it, I don't have the strength to move forward.*

I could feel my inner resolve crumbling with this latest escapade. Somehow, I managed to stay focused and function, going through the motions, though emotionally stuck and unable to socialize with co-workers or get to know my patients beyond their chief complaints. Living in the moment, fearful of moving forward, I barely had the strength to pray.

After I hung up with Karen, my next patient arrived a few minutes later. He was a clean-shaven, serious young man named James. He was well-dressed in casual clothes and sitting quietly on the stretcher in a cubicle as I approached him.

"My throat's been real sore for the past few days, and I'm feeling awful," he said.

After taking the customary history and noting his flaming-red throat on exam, I cultured his throat to rule out streptococcal pharyngitis.

"You have strep throat, so it's good you came in today," I said, after getting the results of the rapid culture test.

"Do you want anything for the pain?" I asked.

Stretching out his arms and fanning his fingers in a "Whoa" position, he shook his head.

"Oh, no. I'm a recovering alcoholic, and I don't want to take any pain medications."

"Really? Tell me your story," I said as I sat down on the stool next to his stretcher, suddenly interested in hearing his side of the story. Pulling the bedside table in front of me, I put my pen down and leaned my chin into my hand to listen.

Without hesitation, he began, 'I started drinking when I was twelve. Then I really got into it by the time I was sixteen."

I shuddered at the parallel to Brian's story and felt pangs of hope for Brian.

He continued to share the details of not only his heavy drinking but also of the many losses he'd experienced as a result.

"I lost my job, my car, my wife, my family, my friends—all gone—and then I almost lost my life in a car accident," he said, looking straight into my eyes.

"So what made you decide to quit?" I said, hanging on to every word and anxious to hear his answer.

"When my wife kicked me out. When she stopped puttin' up with my drinkin'," he said. "I had to decide for myself. Nobody can do it for ya'. And I went to AA. That's my lifeline."

His words and his presence gave me an immediate sense of peace. If James could do it, so could Brian. Brian would have to *want* to get sober, as James did.

"Thanks for sharing your story, James. You're doing the hard work."

"I'm just doing what I have to do, one day at a time."

I handed him an antibiotic prescription. "I hope you feel better. Please follow up with your doctor if your symptoms persist."

James, the patient, had been the one to console me.

Life ebbs and flows, and so does hope. Some days, I felt the hope more strongly than others, but as long as there was life, there was hope. And as long was there hope, miracles could occur. As I listened to James's story, it was clear to me that I was still holding out for that miracle.

My renewed sense of hope carried me to the next patient—I felt lighter. I was now on sacred ground with a power greater than myself leading the way. Even though Brian was still missing and I was still fearful for his life, tapping into my hope that he could recover in time made me feel like we had a fighting chance.

Three days later, I finally heard from Brian. He had been picked up for disturbing the peace and was getting ready to be discharged from jail. Another chance to get his life together again.

CHAPTER 29

No News Is Good News . . . Maybe, 2007

"How's Brian doing? Can he come up to the lake for your vacation week?" Gary, my brother, had asked on the phone when I arrived for my annual week at the family cottage on Keuka Lake in July of 2007. Six months had passed since my son's Christmastime relapse.

"Well, the last time we spoke, two weeks ago, he sounded good. Still working as a vendor, selling leather goods, watches, and jackets and paying his bills. He won't be able to come this year."

I hated that Brian missed our week at the cottage. Leigh Ann, her husband Dave, and my grandsons, Jacob and Ethan, kept me occupied, but Brian's absence was palpable. I tried not to let it overshadow my time with my parents and family. A silent mother's grief took hold of me, and all I could do was ride it out through this annual family vacation and all the family weddings, picnics, and holidays that he missed. I suppose at some point I got used to it because I had no choice. *How does a mother ever get used to a missing alcoholic child?*

For years and months, my child, the addict, was missing, both physically and emotionally, from our lives. It never got easier, but I learned over time to accept that this was part of his disease.

I developed the mantra, "No news is good news," which kept me calm for two or three weeks. By the end of three weeks, if I hadn't heard from him during that particular absence, panic started rising in my throat, and I fought off wild imaginings about his whereabouts and activities.

It was clear that my problems weren't going away. I needed continuing professional help, which I received from a psychologist, Dr. Rudy, who had supported me with the cancer diagnosis and Brian's addiction back in 1999.

"Focus on what he said the last time you spoke with Brian and try not to project your thoughts on Brian's reality. Until you hear of something negative happening, you have no evidence that he isn't doing alright."

I clung to his logic as a way of coping with those fragile moments when I needed something to hang on to that would anchor me through the storm of Brian's bizarre behaviors that landed him either in jail or in an emergency room. It was the only way I could foster hope.

But in my weaker moments, when the negative thoughts seemed to take over, I relapsed into old patterns. Like the day Wayne was sitting across from me at the kitchen table and I said,

"Where is he? What is he doing? What if he starts drinking again? What will become of him?" I droned on in endless chatter during one of Brian's episodes, my heart in a vise. From across the table, Wayne sat quietly.

After listening to my concerns about Brian, Wayne said, "I think it's time for you to go to a meeting." I had missed a few weeks of meetings and knew Wayne was right. It made me realize how important it was for me to work my own program of recovery from co-dependency and enabling, and to nurture my hope, every day.

"I'm not saying it's easy, but as long as Brian knows he's got you worried, he can manipulate you into doing things for him," Wayne said. "You do him no favors by trying to do for him what he should and could be doing for himself." I think Wayne had felt this all along, but this was the first time he verbalized his strong feelings about my enabling Brian. It helped me break through my own denial and start to see the situation in a new light. I knew it was taking me a long time and that I had reached a level of obsession about Brian. As I'd read, a person who is co-dependent relies on another person for happiness. Brian's well-being was my obsession, and it was wearing me down.

I knew that I should be doing more in terms of nurturing my own self-care needs with proper nutrition, exercise, and seeking support. Instead, I had given in to incessant worry over Brian's welfare. It was high time I learned to let go—once and for all.

It was time not just to believe Brian was capable and resourceful but also to learn to let go of my need to step in and do for him what he should be doing for himself. I thought of my letting go in a more positive light. I told myself that my letting go would enable him to find out for himself that he did have the inner strength to tackle his problems. My holding on in my attempt to protect him from his own consequences was delaying this realization. He wouldn't feel a sense of his own empowerment if I was always there, trying to take over.

Once again, Wayne managed to inject his trademark dry sense of humor into the conversation to feed my hope with this reminder:

"Don't worry, Kathy. Brian wouldn't make a good homeless person in the long haul."

Letting go was tested in January 2008, when I experienced acute shortness of breath as I climbed the stairs after a staff meeting at work. After the meeting, I went to my office and sat at my desk until the shortness of breath subsided. Immediately, I made an appointment with my cardiologist for the next day. He scheduled a cardiac catheterization for two days later to identify the cause of my symptoms.

The day of the catheterization, I sat on the stretcher waiting for my turn and thought about all the things I had to do. I figured I would be discharged after the procedure and resume my normal activities at work as a nurse practitioner in primary care. My schedule was busy, and the hours were long, but I was feeling better. I certainly didn't want to miss much time at work.

"Your ejection fraction (indication of heart function) is 10%," Dr. Conn, the doctor who performed the catheterization, said as he looked down on me over his wire-rimmed glasses. "Your heart function is seriously compromised, and you need to be admitted to the hospital for observation and treatment."

"Do you mean I can't go to work on Monday?"

"Your cardiologist, Dr. Barron, will see you on the floor later tonight, and you can discuss this with him."

The hospital was over capacity that night, and I ended up on a stretcher in the hallway until a bed opened up. I was a hospital patient again. Once I was in a room, Dr. Barron walked in.

"Well, now we know why you were short of breath," he said.

"What does this all mean, Dr. Barron?"

"You have cardiomyopathy from the chemotherapy. Thirty percent of patients with this get better, thirty percent stay the same, and thirty percent get worse. We'll adjust your medications, and we'll just have to wait and see where you will fit."

"When can I go back to work?"

"We have to monitor you for at least two weeks on the new medications to see how you respond. In the meantime, take it easy, and don't lift anything heavier than 5 pounds—no laundry baskets, climbing stairs, or anything that will put undue strain on our heart. Your heart needs a rest."

I knew Brian would be upset with the news of my declining heart function, but I had no way to reach him. It fueled my determination to keep fighting and hoping in both our futures.

I stayed in the hospital for two days and then returned home to wait out my treatment and angst over Brian's whereabouts. Karen had called again and said Brian had now been missing for three days. She had told Brian about my hospitalization, but I was never able to talk directly with him. As it turned out, work had become a distraction from worrying about Brian, but I had no escape from the downtime at home. It amounted simply to more time to focus, worry, and feel an immense loss of control, not only over Brian but also over my body and life.

The visions of Brian wandering aimlessly on the streets of New York put my already-stressed heart into crisis mode. Yes, my heart needed a rest from all this stress, too. At one point, while on leave from work and out of desperation, I called Ed, his father.

"Ed, I'm so scared about Brian. Karen called me and said he went missing again three days ago." Ed knew that Brian was dating Karen. "What if he is dead somewhere? What if he has no ID on him, which often happens when he is on a binge? I'm beside myself."

Ed worked as a corrections officer at the time this was happening and knew the penal system in New York State. We differed in our views about dealing with Brian. Ed thought he should just grow up, and I rationalized his behavior as acting out frustrations over his father's relative absence in his life.

"Well, he's probably having a grand old time somewhere while you're working yourself into this panic," Ed said. "Geez, when is he going to grow up?"

"I know—you may be right, but what if he's dead? I can't stand the thought of him lying in a morgue and not being able to identify his body." I was searching for some relief from my pain and worry and working myself up into a frenzy.

"He's in the system, Kath. He's been fingerprinted. They can identify him by the fingerprints."

"Oh, OK. That brings me some consolation. Thanks," I said, realizing my own desperation when a response like that gave me relief. This endless loop of catastrophizing events with Brian was something Dr. Rudy and I had talked about in therapy. I knew it was all part of the co-dependency, guilt, and shame that drove my actions. Until I forgave myself for moving my children all over the country and marrying the wrong men, I would continue to stay in this futile loop.

"I bet he'll turn up soon. Try not to make yourself sick over this," Ed said. His concerned tone consoled me in the moment. At least I felt like we were together in our concern for Brian.

"Thanks, Ed. I'll let you know if I hear anything, and you do the same."

A few nights later, while I was watching television, the phone rang at eleven o'clock. *Who could it be?* I was already restless but immediately sensed some danger. My heart started pounding as I picked up the receiver.

"Ma'am, this is Tony Martino. I'm a New York City police officer. Your son gave me your number. I picked him up in Manhattan. He was shadow boxing under a streetlight, and an elderly lady looking out her window got nervous and called us."

"Where is he? Is he okay?" I said, pressing my hand to my chest.

"He needs help. I took him to the emergency room for a psychiatric evaluation. Here is the number to call."

"Thank you so much for calling. I've been worried about him. He does need help."

"You're welcome, ma'am. He seems like a nice young man. I hope he gets the help he needs."

When I called the emergency room, they informed me that he had signed himself out and that they couldn't hold him against his will. My relief was short-lived.

Prayer helped me navigate the rocky feelings of mothering an addict. Once again Doctor Rudy's voice kept me grounded. "You have no tangible evidence that anything bad is happening." *No news is good news.* But then again, was it not? At least I knew he was alive. That would have to be hope enough.

Three days later, after being released from jail for disturbing the peace, Brian phoned me, sounding contrite and weary.

"I got picked up a few nights ago for loitering in a no-trespassing zone, Mom," Brian said. This was a different episode from the initial one involving the police.

"Mom. Are you alright?"

"I am now."

I was back to work three weeks after this episode.

CHAPTER 30

A Mother's Trap, 2008

A month later, on a cold, gloomy, and dismal February afternoon in 2008, Brian called with a plea: rent money.

His litany of pleas and promises made me cringe. My gut tightened even more when he started promising me he'd go back to Alcoholics Anonymous, work, theater, and baseball. How I wanted to call him out on them all. I had reached my breaking point with him and myself.

"I've done it before, Mom, and I will do it again," he pleaded.

"I know, Brian. We both know what you are capable of," I said, trying to stay levelheaded and calm. Anger seethed just below the surface, but the guilt and shame that had plagued me for years kept me from unleashing it on Brian.

His pleas became bait. And there I was, tugged like a fish on a hook. I knew deep in my heart that I shouldn't pay his rent. But I did, telling him that this would be the last time. Just a month before, I had wired him $1000—again. I couldn't bear to see him homeless. My son. And just like that, Karen had called me in tears that he was missing on that gloomy February day. It finally dawned on me that this was how I was hurting him, not helping him. The money was certainly not helping him take responsibility. I panicked, filled with a sense of regret, only after I'd mailed the check with his latest request. If only I had trusted my inner wisdom and hadn't mailed the latest check, I might have saved myself and him from more regret and heartache.

What is it about our children that our own suffering pales in comparison to whatever event is happening in their lives? Brian's heartache and pain were unbearable to me, though I could only speculate as to the reason he drank. *Was he "trying to emulate" his dad or fill the void left by his dad's absence? Is that why he drank?* Meanwhile, I still carried the guilt of not providing my children with a stable family life. I can see in retrospect that at this time I was still deeply entrenched in my need to step in and rescue my son. I was the classic co-dependent, the enabler, repeating the drill of trying to save my son, the addict, from himself, at my own expense, despite the predictable consequences. I was trapped by my own need to mother him.

Karen called me occasionally and told me that she had been refusing Brian's calls. Though I understood, I felt sad for the loss of their relationship, but I respected her need to set healthy boundaries. That was something I needed to work on for myself, too. But I had to pull back and try even harder not to get involved.

I had grown close to Karen through the ups and downs of their relationship over the past two years, carefully trying to share Al-Anon principles with her. *How does one live with an addict, sober or drinking?* The love is there, but the disease is, too, rearing up in subtle and blatant ways. When Brian was sober, I became complacent about following Al-Anon. I had forgotten that his disease was always lurking close by, eager to go into action at any given time. I couldn't imagine what it must have been like for Brian, constantly having to negotiate his way around such an ominous presence.

CHAPTER 31

Awakening, 2009

For years, Brian had been a high priority, while I continued to neglect my own needs. It would take me years before I started making my own needs a priority. I realized that, no matter what I did, Brian, now thirty-four, was making his own decisions. It was an uphill battle that had left me exhausted, frustrated, and fighting despair. Scenes from the past reminded me of the repercussions of addiction for all of us.

After so many years of waiting and worrying, the time had come for me to save myself. *How could I let go of my son without giving up on him?* My enabling behavior was dragging us both down. The time had come for me to break my addiction to Brian's addiction and to my own suffering. And so, in February of 2009, I decided to take personal responsibility for my actions and show up with my vulnerable self at a nearby Dominican retreat center, where I had attended a women's weekend retreat for the past five years.

A modest-looking one-story building that had previously served as a convent sat back from a busy highway, surrounded by trees and shrubbery, as if to shield it from the hustle and bustle of daily life. This annual women's weekend retreat was an oasis in the desert—an entire weekend of solitude, prayer, and stepping away from the chaos and angst of the everyday life to which I had become accustomed. It left me feeling refreshed and renewed. For years, the focus had always been on Brian. Every prayer, counseling session, conversation, and ritual involved my hope for his recovery from his ugly addiction.

And for years, nothing had really changed, despite all my prayerful pleas. Brian moved into and out of recovery as predictably as the seasons changed. All my thoughts and efforts went toward trying to control his life, and I was paying a high price for neglecting my own needs.

While sitting in my room at the retreat, I recalled the scene in my family room back in 2000, when the story of USS *Cole* terror attack flashed across the TV screen. The naval ship had docked at Yemen to refuel and was attacked by several suicide bombers, later identified as Al Qaeda fighters. Seventeen US sailors were killed and thirty-nine injured. As I stared at the screen, frozen in place, I thought how Brian was just as lost to me as those young sailors were to their mothers. At that time, Brian was between halfway houses. At that moment, I did not know his whereabouts, and a sense of impending doom washed over me. I pondered what would become of my son, as I often did when I knew addiction had taken over and once again left me feeling empty and helpless.

How would I let go of my son, yet still not give up on him? It was a battle I fought with myself every day until I decided to fully take responsibility for my actions and claim my vulnerability when the date for the retreat rolled around in February of 2009.

I was his cheerleader, the one who never gave up hope for him when everyone else seemed to shake their heads in resignation over the prospects of his ever getting better. I steadfastly clung to hope when everyone doubted his ability to ever recover. Being his mother and his advocate strengthened me to keep fighting.

"He needs tough love." "You need to be stronger." "Why do you think he drinks?" well-meaning family and friends would say to me in their attempt to offer support. The litany only made me feel worse about myself, like I had failed him by not being tough enough or not understanding why he drank.

And while Brian was in and out of recovery, I was still holding out for sustaining long-term results. I had learned from years of trial and error supporting Brian that recovery is a process, a journey—not a quick fix.

In my journal writing from this retreat, I poured out my weariness on the pages, pleading with God to strengthen me for this battle as I sat in my room.

> *Dear God, I come to be refreshed, renewed in mind, body, and spirit. I am weary from the distractions and worries over Brian and my health. Fill*

me up with your peace—the peace of knowing and trusting that You are the great miracle maker. For I do believe my son's addiction and my addiction to his addiction will require a miracle to overcome.

During the opening session on Friday night, Sister Eleanor, the retreat director, encouraged us to "go where the spirit of God takes you."

We all listened as she continued. "God wants you to be the fullness of what you can be. Allow Him to enter into you. All God needs is your desire. He loves you just the way you are."

I was mesmerized by her message and very ready to receive her direction.

Sister Eleanor then led us in a guided meditation, where we visualized going down to a pond and bathing ourselves in the healing waters. I envisioned myself walking slowly but expectantly. I was desperate for relief from the years of heartache and burdens of watching Brian destroy his life, missing many opportunities to grow, because of his addiction to alcohol.

When we returned from the pond, she directed us to write down our worries on a piece of paper and place them in a bowl on the altar. As we sat in the silence of the darkened chapel, she lit a match to the pile and let them burn, the furls of smoke taking our deepest concerns away.

I knew in order to fully trust this message, I needed to let go of my need to control. Turning him away that snowy night in 2002 was seared in my memory as an ultimate act of faith and love. And yet it was an agonizing reminder of what is required when one's child is an addict. It went against every fiber of what I felt a mother should be—firm but loving. I hated it, but I also knew it was his only chance—and my only choice.

During the retreat, I was soothed hearing a stanza from the *Let Your God Love You* poem by Edward Gately:

"Be still before God.

Be still.

Let your God look upon you with enormous love."

I would soon learn from embracing the bigger concept of letting go at the retreat that divine intervention seemed like the most logical option. Although support-group meetings, counseling, and journaling helped, I still struggled with not being able to help him. *How do I keep loving my son but not allow his disease to permeate my heart, soul, and spirit?*

My love for Brian has always been fierce, unrestrained, unconditional, deeply in tune with my heart and soul. But my mother's heart at the time of the retreat and for many years before was broken, stirred by the need to take responsibility for all his problems, even when it came time to giving him second, third, and fourth chances. But it ended up crippling him with lying, manipulating, and self-serving behaviors. I had to find a way to get past the anger and the pain of regret that ate away at my own self-esteem to do good by Brian.

I thought about all the times in the past when Brian had repeated, "Mom, I'm really working hard, going to meetings, and staying sober. I need rent money and maybe a little extra for food. I promise to pay you back."

Instead of screaming, I tried to respond calmly, even though I wasn't feeling calm inside. "Brian, your history does not make me trust you. I can no longer give you money only to have you relapse again and again."

"I know, Mom. I don't blame you," he said one day, sounding genuinely understanding.

I often wondered what would happen if I unleashed my anger on him. Perhaps he would be so startled by the change in my behavior that he would take note. I realized I'd never learned how to express anger in a healthy way. Ours was a household where I never heard my parents argue and "fight" openly. Rather, silence was the expected response. There were many family dinners where my siblings and I sat in collective discomfort shifting our gazes between Dad and Mom, who sat stoically at either end of the table. It was easier to stuff it inside, but, clearly, that wasn't working now. I was happy that, over the years, both my parents began expressing themselves more openly. I would need to find a way to negotiate my way around the underlying anger associated with Brian's behavior.

Contrary to the past, when I felt defeated, torn, and furious that I was allowing myself to be manipulated again, there was a flicker of hope in my heart that signaled that maybe this time helping him would help him get on his way. But the battle raged inside my head. *When is helping enabling?* I wrote the check to his landlord, and, as soon as I'd sent it, I knew in my heart it was not helping. More often than not, I was right.

I knew there was no magical fix for my problems. I still had a lot of work to do to achieve healthy boundaries for

Brian and me. But it became clearer to me that letting go did not mean giving up. The love of my son was intact. It was my addiction to his addiction that I needed to let go.

The retreat set a new stage for me to move from, one in which I learned to focus on my own recovery.

CHAPTER 32

Relapse Is Part of Recovery, 2010

A mother's heart beats for her child even when her child does outrageous things, like the time he called me from a bar, in December of 2009, when he lived in New York City.

"Hey, Mom," he said, his voice high-pitched and tense.

"Hi, B. Where are you?" I hadn't heard from him in a month. I knew immediately that he was drinking by his fast-paced speech.

"Ah, I'm in midtown Manhattan." He paused. "I need to ask a favor."

The muffled voices in the background and the assumption that he was at a bar left me feeling manipulated before I even heard his request. I took a deep breath and reminded myself that I did not want to remain addicted to his addiction.

"Can you pay my $183 bar tab? I have no money."

"No." I thought of the Al-Anon phrase about saying "No" as a complete sentence. Let him take responsibility for this.

"Well, I guess I'll just have to be arrested," he said, smugly.

At that moment, I was done with the lectures and the pleas, fed up with his empty promises and attempts to serve as his buffer against the consequences of his behavior. He had become a menace to society. I allowed myself to stay with my anger, despite my heartache that he had reached this new low. I could not continue caving to his requests and then be left to suffer the consequences of his misdeeds.

"I suppose you will."

"Thanks a lot, Mom," he said, sarcastically and sullen—as if he were pulling out all stops, hoping I would cave. Blood rushed to my face. I felt furious that he was putting me in this position of having to choose between stepping in and letting go.

"I love you, B, but I won't keep bailing you out when you're the one who keeps getting yourself into these fixes," I said, resolving to stand firm.

As I looked at the phone after hanging up from his call requesting money, I wondered if my decision not to bail out my son would lead to an even more serious relapse that would shadow any kind of future hope for his recovery. After all, I had yet to witness a long-term period of recovery.

"One of these days it will work," he had said after one of his rehab programs in 2003.

Now, more than ever, I needed to trust and believe that Brian would learn something valuable from this relapse.

The good news was that, in the past, he had been open to treatment, though some rehab admissions were court-appointed, and that he was still alive. He had a will to live. And where there's life, there's hope.

A year later, in November of 2010, I held vigil at my eighty-eight-year-old father's bedside. He had suffered a brainstem stroke and had been placed in comfort care. I sat rubbing his swollen arm and worn hands, telling him how much I loved him. His skin was pink and soft, and felt warm against my hand. I held his hand and stroked his fingers. His nails were smooth and trimmed, as they had always been. The wrinkles had been ironed out by the swelling. These were the hands that had guided me through tenth-grade geometry, through setting up a personal budget. Those hands had held mine as we walked down the aisle and danced the father-daughter dance at my wedding to Wayne in 2001. Now, they dropped motionless atop the pillows under his arms. How blessed I've been to have such a wonderful father. And knowing this still deepened my grief for my children, whose father had been absent to them.

At the time, Brian was still in New York City, and, though I didn't know how he was doing on a day-to-day basis, I knew he needed to know about his grandfather. Grandpa understood Brian, as he had gone through his own rebellious period when his widowed father brought home his new stepmother, leaving Dad and his three older siblings stunned at the time. He supported Brian throughout high school by cheering for him at his baseball games, by being a strong male role model when Brian's dad was not available. They enjoyed a special bond, as Grandpa understood Brian's errant ways, even though he did not understand or condone his drinking.

As I sat by Dad's bedside, I reached for my cell phone and called Brian's number, not knowing the status of his recovery. I was relieved when he answered on the second ring, as he'd often let the calls go to voicemail.

"Hi, B. I have some bad news."

"Oh, no, Mom. What?"

"Grandpa had a stroke, and he's not expected to live."

"What?" he said, sounding confused.

"Yes. It happened two days ago. I tried to reach you before, but there was no answer."

Silence.

"B, if I hold the phone up to Grandpa's ear, can you talk to him?"

"Geez, Mom. I don't know what to say."

He sounded irritated and frazzled.

"I don't even know how I feel right now."

"You can just say goodbye and tell him you love him."

The mother in me wanted Brian to have a chance to say goodbye without regrets, and, yet, he was resisting me, but, still, I persisted. Without a moment's hesitation, I held the phone to Dad's ear and said, "Go ahead, B."

I don't know what he said or if he said anything. When I got back on the phone minutes later, he told me how uncomfortable I'd made him feel. The edge in his voice clued me in that he might be drinking, but I felt consoled that at least I gave him a chance to say goodbye.

"Why are you doing this to me, Mom?" he shouted.

I brushed off my uneasy feeling that—based on his angry tones—he was probably using. If he were sober, he would have been grieving over the loss of his grandpa, not blaming me for upsetting him.

Dad died, two days later, on the day after Thanksgiving, and Brian made plans to come to Corning on the bus for the funeral.

On the day I was supposed to pick him up at the bus station, the phone rang. It was Karen.

"Brian won't be coming. He's been drinking and smoking marijuana for a few weeks and doesn't have any money." I thought Karen had severed her ties with Brian, but she was still in and out of his life, unable to fully let go and move on.

Even though I could have justified buying his bus ticket for this reason, I knew he was in no condition to attend the funeral.

Accepting that Brian would not be able to attend his grandpa's funeral was excruciating. It went against the grain of how I envisioned my role as his mother. I carried him in my womb for nine months, nurturing, giving, and sacrificing, just as most mothers would. It was my job to ease his pain and make his life better, but he didn't seem to understand how important it was to show up and pay his respects for a person who had supported him for so long. But he was too entrenched in his drinking to see this.

This was a true test of my ability to help him understand how important family is. But at that moment, it became clearer to me that I had no control over his mental crutches of manipulations, lies, and self-destructive behavior. When we bid Dad farewell, I added the loss of my son who was still alive to the loss of Dad, and my need to control Brian's life went with him.

CHAPTER 33

The Roller Coaster Ride of Addiction, 2012

Brian's absences from my life continued to keep me on edge, as I was always on guard for his next relapse. It was impossible to suddenly become numb to my feelings. When I reached my three-week limit of not hearing from him, in August of 2012, nearly two years after Dad's funeral, I tried unsuccessfully to reach him on his cell phone.

I could only imagine that he was gone again. Wasted. Plunged into the depths of despair. Alcohol and marijuana-saturated. The sporadic phone calls prior to this relapse gave me no clear indication at the time that he was drinking, but I knew the unpredictable nature of his disease. He sounded sober and level-headed, though he spoke of struggling about the direction he should be taking. At thirty-seven, he was still living in New York City and working as a street vendor.

"Tony, my boss, calls me 'Wonder Boy' because I can really turn the merchandise," he told me a few weeks before on the phone "But Mom, being on the streets is starting to mess with my mind."

I knew he was itching for a change, but we both knew his job options were severely limited by his lack of a college education.

He was seeing an outpatient counselor until six weeks prior to his relapse, when he called me in tears. Usually when Brian was in tears, it could mean only that he had been drinking. But this time, he sounded sober.

"Mom, I have to read you the letter Dad sent me."

A letter from his father? I closed my eyes and breathed in a sigh of relief at the thought of Ed reaching out to Brian. Ed and Brian spoke sporadically throughout the years, but Ed rarely reached out to Brian.

It turned out that his dad had poured out his feelings in this letter, something that he rarely did, even in our marriage, and his words of love and fatherly advice about life, women, and career choices. This letter was huge.

"Mom, this means so much to me," Brian said, as he rapidly read me his dad's words, stopping to catch his breath in between sentences. *Brian had craved a relationship with his dad for many years. Could this be the beginning of that?*

The excitement in his voice was contagious, and I envisioned Brian's eyes lighting up as he read. My heart was filled with gratitude and hope that Ed had finally stepped up to the plate after being relatively absent from Brian's life since the divorce in 1977. In my mind, he never did fulfill his fatherly duties with his sporadic visits. But the kids loved him, and I tried to be supportive of his role as their father, often times through clenched teeth. I grieved for my children and the lack of a strong fatherly presence in their lives. My father was a strong role model. I chose to feel reassured that Brian and his dad would begin to forge a meaningful bond, a bond that would hopefully help Brian fill the hole in his heart.

Six weeks later, the cell phone lying on my desk vibrated and flashed an unfamiliar number. I entertained not answering it, but the New York City area code lured me to swipe the green answer strip. The voice on the other end was calm and friendly, though it was no one I recognized.

"Hi. I'm calling about Brian. Are you his mom?"

"Yes, I am." My heart started racing as I braced myself for whatever news awaited me.

"I'm Spencer Willis, one of Brian's roommates, but you can call me Spence. How are you?"

After filling me in on the dreaded details of Brian's recent substance-induced escapades—throwing items into the aisles in a local supermarket—he finally told me what I didn't want to hear: the landlord had decided to evict Brian. My heart sunk at these words as I braced myself for another period of uncertainty. Brian was homeless again in New York City.

"We've cleaned his room. I won't go into the details, but it was a mess, pretty much a reflection of the space he was in."

As hard as this was to hear, the compassion and sorrow in the voice of this messenger uplifted me in the moment.

We made arrangements to rent a storage unit that I agreed to pay for and into which he agreed to move Brian's belongings with the help of the two other roommates.

"You are a very compassionate young man, Spence, and I am grateful for what you and your other roommates are doing."

"Thanks. We wish Brian the best and hope he remains the strong and creative person he is. He's a great guy, and we know he needs help."

How many times had I heard that my son needs help? But this time, I didn't feel alone in my compassion for my son. I felt relieved to know that someone else beyond my world of doctors and nurses actually cared.

Brian's worldly possessions now fit into a 5' x 9' storage bin with room to spare. I wondered how long it would be before Brian moved to another place.

Spence gave me the number of the VA hospital unit where Brian had been admitted and told me he had talked with Brian. We ended the conversation with the hope that Brian would get the help he needs and be able to move on in his life.

As I dialed the number, an unexpected sense of peace flowed through me.

"Tell me what I need to hear, B," I said over the phone, weary and resigned. I hoped he had picked up the resignation in my voice. I had run out of things to say and resources to help.

"That I've hit bottom," he said, his voice strong and clear. "I've agreed to start medication, too."

In the twenty-three years since Brian had started drinking, I'd never heard those words from him—the words I longed to hear, the place he needed to reach: "I've hit bottom."

I allowed those words to buoy me as I reminded myself of the kindness of Spence, who looked past Brian's offensive behavior and into the heart of my son. I had been waiting for twenty-three years. Perhaps this was the sign I needed to know that Brian was finally on his way. It was as if God had sent me a messenger of hope to help me endure the days of waiting and wondering that followed his downfall.

CHAPTER 34

Accepting a New Normal, 2011–2013

As Brian continued to struggle with his addiction, I continued to focus on my own recovery from his addiction, sending him cards and letters, going to support meetings, and generally trying to live one day at a time. More than ever, I craved normal, and anything that helped me recapture a childhood memory took me back there, before the chaos of addiction entered my world. The memories of my life before addiction were a welcome relief from the constant worry and heartache over Brian. So, I imagined a life without worries and anxieties. It felt liberating to think there would be happier days ahead.

But dealing with Brian usually put me in crisis mode. I wanted more from my life. I didn't want to feel like a dishrag—tired and worn out. I wanted to be able to enjoy my life and health freely and with vigor for as long as I was physically able.

Despite my own misgivings about retiring from a forty-four-year nursing career I loved, I had to create a new normal for myself. So, in August 2011, I tearfully hugged my patients goodbye and began planning for a long-awaited trip to Italy to visit my maternal grandfather's family in a small mountain village east of Naples known as Dugenta—an opportunity to materialize deeper connections from girlhood. From age seven until the end of high school, I spent entire summers in Schenectady, New York, with my maternal grandparents, Carmella, otherwise known as "Nan," and Alfredo DiCerbo. Grandpa had come over from Dugenta on the USS *Calabria* out of Naples in 1900 with his brother Vincenzo. His family farmed tomatoes and grapes, but Alfredo and Vincenzo wanted to find more lucrative work in America. They sold their portion of the farm to relatives and took off for the land of opportunity.

In the months leading up to the trip, Wayne and I listened to tapes and practiced speaking common Italian phrases, often times laughing at our awkward speech. Knowing I'd soon be able to put to use some of my Italian with members of the family fueled my sense of curiosity. *What did they look like? Would they know who I was?* We had never met, but Grandpa used to send family pictures in with his letters.

I contacted the limousine service that Uncle Michael, my mother's brother, had raved about, and remained in close communication with Barbara, the secretary who helped me contact the family by letter. We would arrive on Friday, September 13, 2013. Uncle Michael had traveled to Dugenta with his wife, children, and grandchildren in 2009. The family had greeted him with open arms. I envisioned the same warm homecoming with our trip.

Till this day, the happy memories of Grandpa DiCerbo's kindness and fun-loving nature make me smile. I had always visualized him sitting on the back porch in the dark on stifling summer nights listening to his beloved Yankees on the radio and spewing out his reactions in Italian. He also loved Chester from the TV show *Gunsmoke*. He shot up from his chair during a commercial and mimicked Chester's limp, laughing as his gold-capped tooth glistened. These warm memories reminded me of my happy childhood, when a loving family surrounded me. The opportunity to connect with Grandpa's family helped me to reconnect with that feeling of warmth and security at a time when my peace of mind was threatened. I had never been so far away from home, so I felt sporadic pangs of anxiety over leaving Brian for the two weeks we'd be gone. But my awareness that letting go of not being able to control Brian's behavior allowed me to concentrate on enjoying my life in the here and now.

My favorite memory when I was ten years old is of Grandpa's excitement when he received a letter from his family along with updates and pictures from "the old country." When he started rattling something off in Italian, eyes wide and hands flailing, I felt his joy, though I didn't understand a word he was saying. I wanted to re-experience that joy, that child-like wonder, again.

I often wondered how difficult it must have been for him to leave his family at the age of sixteen and never see them again. Mom's brother and sister, my Uncle Michael and Aunt Rose, had traveled to Italy with their families and visited with the extended family several times, bringing back pictures and tales of standing in the bedroom where Grandpa was born. They were greeted with warmth and love. But as the years waned, I, too, wanted to get to know my Italian side of the family, to reconnect with those happy memories. I was hopeful that reconnecting with these memories would help me stand firmer in my new normal.

In 2013, Wayne and I traveled to Rome, Pompeii, the Amalfi Coast, Florence, and Venice—all spectacular sights to behold. However, nothing could compare to the experience of connecting with Dugenta, Grandpa's birthplace, and the family he loved so dearly.

Maurizio, our translator and driver, picked us up at seven-thirty in the morning on Friday, September 13, at the hotel in Sorrento and drove Wayne and me through the windy, narrow mountain roads of Southern Italy. As we passed the sign for Dugenta for the first time, my heart started pounding when Maurizio said, "Here is the home of your grandfather." That was when the tears started coming, for this place had come alive only in my imagination as a child, but to be present and know that Grandpa had walked these roads as a young man was overwhelming.

Maurizio slowly drove around the curvy, steep main road and found the entrance to the complex where Grandpa's family lived. Along the rows of stucco houses separated by alleyways, two young boys playing kickball in front of one of the houses reminded me of a *National Geographic* photo of an Italian village.

Grandpa's eighty-five-year-old niece, Maria, one of Grandpa's five nieces and nephews, greeted us from her second-floor window, flagging Wayne, Maurizio, and me down as we wandered around the alleyways between the stucco houses. She motioned us from the top of the stairs, and we trudged up, stepping onto the landing. As I stepped into the kitchen at the top of the stairs, I looked over and saw a plate of cookies on the kitchen table. Old photos of relatives adorned the walls. A seat cushion with the embroidered words "Lake George" caught my eye and reminded me of home. Grandpa or Uncle Vincent had probably sent that gift. Seeing that cushion in this faraway place that I had only imagined for years made me feel even more connected, knowing that something from my hometown had made it over to Maria's kitchen.

Maria took us on a tour of her apartment, leading us into the bedroom and showing us the bed where my grandfather was born. She gathered some snapshots of Grandpa and Uncle Vincent right before they left for America and then said in Italian, with tears in her eyes, "You never forget." Maria was the daughter of Grandpa's youngest sister, Anna, and hadn't even been born when Grandpa left. The family ties were that strong.

Soon Maria spoke on the phone with the other relatives who instructed us to walk down the lane to Vittorio and Marie's house—past the fig and kiwi trees, past the goats and chickens in the wire-fenced-in yards—where we were ushered into the kitchen as younger women of the family scurried around serving us fruit juice and offering us cookies.

I had fun practicing my Italian. "Alfredo was my *nonno*," I said as I pulled out the snapshot of Grandpa and me at Christmas when I was a toddler. Then I showed pictures of my children. Brian stood handsome and smiling in the picture I chose to share, proof of better days that I hoped would return. For that moment, I almost forgot that he had a drinking problem and basked in the glow of showing off my handsome son. My American son Brian. Not the drinker. Or the alcoholic. These were details I did not want to share with my newfound Italian family. From the other side of the Atlantic Ocean, I wanted to remember Brian in a more complete and joyful way. As much as thinking about Brian's drinking filled me with shame, I continued to anchor him in a positive way, and that meant connecting with him from a more joyful place within my family.

After a short visit at Vittorio's and Marie's house, we were off again to our final destination at Luigi's and Louise's, which appeared to be the main gathering place for the family. It was the largest home in the complex, and we gathered around a long dining-room table as relatives of all ages streamed in and joined us around the table. Our tour guide, Maurizio, was kept very busy trying to translate as everyone chattered at once. At one point, he turned to me and said,

"Luigi is telling you that, on the holidays, they have a tradition of opening the window and raising their glasses of homemade *strega*, an Italian liqueur made from grape stems, to send their blessings to their *famiglia* in America. *Salute!*" A warmth surged through my body as I envisioned this ritual.

Luigi was holding out his glass toward the open window, which overlooked a lush vineyard. Relatives brought flowers, baseball caps, bottles of liquor, framed pictures of their families. Then, Luigi invited us to stay for a meal. I looked over at Maurizio, and he nodded, "You have a wonderful family. That's fine." It meant extending the time, but I wasn't going to miss out on a real Italian feast. Six courses—pasta, sausage and peppers, salad, roast beef, figs, nectarines, and wine from the region. Then, when they brought out the homemade *tiramisu*, Wayne held up his hands. I leaned over and whispered,

"You never refuse anything at an Italian table."

I recalled the feeling of fullness I experienced as a child, when my Nan would look over at me and say, "Just try a little bite."

If I closed my eyes, I was ten years old again, enjoying the warmth, laughter, and nonstop banter that was all part of the family I came from. Brian was part of the same family, and I would never give up hope that those strong, loving genes flowing through him would somehow counteract all the forces of addiction.

With a full belly and heart, Maurizio led us back toward the entrance, to our vehicle, and, as we sped off, I pondered the cross-cultural connections I had made during the day.

This trip to the land of my grandfather was a gift I gave to myself, an opportunity to honor my childhood memories, reconnect with my roots, and nurture myself, giving me strength to move forward. If I stood strong in my recovery, maybe Brian would be able to stay strong in his recovery. I chose to believe in that possibility.

CHAPTER 35

Hope Returns, November 2013

I had just finished the same letter I'd written to Brian on the train from Philadelphia, where I'd presented a workshop on journaling for the Women's Writing Circle. When I read the letter, inspired by the writing prompt to the group, I felt encouraged to read it to Brian.

I hadn't seen him in eighteen months because of another relapse during the summer of 2013, four months before our Italian tour, which led him to find his way to a VA housing rehabilitation program known as The Reality House. In a June 2013 phone call from his landlady, she said,

"He tore up the apartment, and we had to call an ambulance to get him away from us."

I could only imagine the physical and emotional devastation he had caused for others, and I relived my own personal hell with each phone call. Like countless other times when he'd relapsed, I turned numb. What more could I say or do? Sporadic phone calls, the negative talk, the anger reminded me of the same warning signs. Inevitably, he'd find his way, followed by detox and rehab, leading me to hope that this relapse would be the last. But now I felt depleted. I hated to admit it, but I felt like it was the end of the line for me.

This time, Brian had found his way into a VA housing rehab program, The Reality House. He was still living at The Reality House when we made arrangements to meet at Penn Station in November. As I walked along the station intently looking for Brian, I was cognizant of the fact that he was still at The Reality House. I struggled with the idea that he may not be receptive to seeing me and whether I would be able to handle his condition. As passengers flurried by, I pondered the idea of sharing the letter I'd written about my deepest feelings and hopes for him. I wanted him to hear my words.

I was nervous, wondering if he'd show and if he did, what condition he'd be in. I didn't know if I'd read him the letter, even though I felt the need to share my feelings with him.

Brian was nowhere in sight. I could feel the anxiety well up in me as I tried to counteract my negative projections that he might not show. A group of giddy young adults gathered in front of me, hugging and laughing, and with each round of laughter, I allowed myself to envision Brian surrounded with friends.

Just at that moment, a familiar shape emerged from the crowd in the distance. Did I dare to believe it was him? How desperately I wanted to know he was alright.

My heart pounded, and my breath quickened as I was reminded of my own words "with fierce mother love, I hold on to hope that you will see yourself as I see you—healthy, whole, and still filled with promise."

Yes, it was him! When I finally saw my smiling, clear-eyed son just like I had envisioned, I grabbed my luggage and hurried to greet him. His arms extended wide. He greeted me with a warm hug, and I melted into his chest, uplifted in the moment and filled with hope.

"Let me look at you, B," I said, gazing up into his dark eyes. I liked what I saw—a straight, steady look back confirmed my greatest expectation that he was sober.

"It's been so long, B," I said. "It's wonderful to see you. You look good."

"Hey, you're looking great, too. I'm doing OK, Mom," he said. "Still struggling, but I'm pushing forward."

I wondered if this was a turning point for him—if he had decided once and for all to stop drinking.

"We need to catch up. Let's find a place to eat, and you can tell me what's going on."

We slid into a booth at one of the restaurants at Penn Station and updated each other on events from the last eighteen months. He shared his experience at The Reality House, noting how he still struggled on a day-to-day basis but that he was fighting to stay on track. I was getting the sense that he was taking responsibility for his actions as my heart ached for his struggles. But I felt consoled that he was sitting in front of me, sober and in reality, very grateful that he was working hard to get his life back on track.

As he talked, right then and there, I pulled out the letter I had written in the workshop and read it to him.

"I have something I'd like to share with you, B," I said as I began reading the letter.

As I read the words, "when I see you, I see. . . .," I looked up and saw that he had tears welling up in his eyes. My own eyes also welled up. The words from my heart were touching his heart.

> *With fierce mother love, I hang on to hope—hope that you will reconnect with that little boy within who has much innate goodness and worth; hope that you will begin to see yourself as I see you—healthy, whole, and still filled with promise.*

We gazed at one another through tear-filled eyes, locked in a moment of silence. Brian reached across the table, held my hands, and said,

"I do have hope, Mom."

In that moment of shared hope, I envisioned us both forging a new path together somewhere along the way, where Brian took care of his own business, and I, his mother, relinquished my need to step in.

"You're an adult now, Brian, and I believe you have the strength within to find your way."

He nodded in response.

When we left the booth and he walked me to my train, I felt like we were on new ground.

CHAPTER 36

Bittersweet Goodbye, 2014

The rest of 2013 and 2014 were uneventful. As Brian continued to make steady progress with his sobriety, meaning frequent phone calls home, sane conversations, and gainful employment, I, too, began settling into a more peaceful and sane state of mind. He even switched from working as a street vendor to an office job, as he felt "being on the streets messed with his head."

Brian was an achiever, but I had worried how he would fare now that he had wasted many of his younger years. He had shown me since he was a child that he could do anything he set his mind to do, such as hold out for the right Matchbox car or win that batting award as a freshman in high school. Witnessing how Brian started to embrace his own inner strength reminded me of the importance of being compassionate about myself. I wasn't sure what had made the difference for him and assumed that he finally had made up his mind to get sober.

While at Mass a few months before publishing my first memoir about my journey into and out of two emotionally abusive marriages, I gave myself permission to reconnect with my younger self from a place of deep compassion. I hadn't felt that way about the decisions I had made with my two marriages for years, and it occurred to me that the time had come to tell myself a different story about my painful past instead of judging myself. The message I received was "You must tell your story for others." I didn't hear voices, only a deep knowing that The Holy Spirit had touched my soul, and I decided to move forward with publishing it.

It was only when I started writing the sketches of what appeared to be a memoir, my first book, in 2009, that I realized the compassion that had brought me to the written page about connecting with the younger woman who had suffered so much abuse. I was torn over what story to tell. Should I tell the story about my abusive marriages or my son's alcohol addiction? As time went on, I found myself writing about the marriages, leading me to believe that I was in greater need of healing.

When the time came to publish my first memoir to the world in 2014, I had questioned whether I was qualified enough to even write this book and how credible my healing journey was. Endless hours spent worrying how Ed and his second wife, Jean, would respond to my story about his drinking occupied my thoughts to the point that I wasn't sure I could publish it. I even consulted an attorney and prayed about it.

I also worried about the effect the story would have on my children. Up until a few months before publication, I wondered if I could or should send such an intimate family story out into the world. I wasn't aware how much courage it would take to tell such an emotional family story. But my passion to share my hope with others who had endured similar circumstances won out.

Finally, I mustered the courage, in July 2014, to publish my first memoir, *Ever Faithful to His Lead: My Journey Away From Emotional Abuse.*

Soon after, we received word that Ed was ill. He didn't want to tell the kids until his wife Jean insisted. It turned out that Ed had end-stage cirrhosis, and, by the time we found out about it, he had been getting progressively worse.

He was still conscious when Leigh and her family and Brian and I visited him for the first time in August 2014. Though his body was swollen, he still had his sense of humor and wits about him, which comforted me. I was still on my guard. I wasn't sure how I would be greeted or if I should even walk into his room. I was prepared to let Brian go in and then wait in the waiting room. But as soon as Ed and Jean saw us at the door, they motioned us in and held out their arms to hug us. I thought of how he had finally reached out to Brian in a letter. Maybe underneath all the chaos of his alcohol addiction was the caring man I had married in 1971, a father who loved his children. Unfortunately, his drinking interfered with his ability to be present to his children.

Jean and I left the room to let father and son have some precious one-on-one time. We stood in the hallway, and Jean shared her grief and sorrow with me. Jean and I had always had a good relationship, but we kept our distance from one another.

Now, words of healing came to me as I absorbed her sorrow. "Jean, I was not the love of Ed's life. You are."

It was my attempt to find some peace after years of turmoil and conflict associated with Ed.

We hugged, and she left for a few hours. We both sensed a need for Brian to be alone with his father, for we had no idea what the next day would bring. And for the next three hours, Brian and Ed connected, probably more time than they had ever spent together over the last twenty years. I realized that this, their time together as death lingered at the door, was the greatest gift they could possibly give each other.

Then a few weeks later, in early August 2014, after returning from Mass with my grandsons in Niskayuna, where we had prayed for Pa-Pa Ed's healing and recovery, Leigh Ann greeted us at the door of her home. Leigh Ann had confronted Ed during her college years in 1994 and had enjoyed a renewed relationship with her father ever since. She was sobbing as we walked in the door.

"This is it," she said, after getting a phone call from Jean's sister. "Dad is dying."

I hugged her, urging her to take the two-hour trip to Syracuse without worrying about her kids.

I called Brian right away and prayed he could get back from New York City in time. He came that night by Amtrak, and promptly the next morning, we drove two hours to Syracuse.

As Brian and I approached Ed's hospital room the next day, Jean walked out of the room, crying. She had just met with the palliative-care team about end-of-life care. Ed was losing consciousness, although he was in and out. We walked slowly into his room and looked upon Ed's large body in bed. Lying still, he began to moan. As I usually did, I stayed to the side, letting Brian first approach his father's bedside.

Brian stood by his bed and put his hand on his father's arm, blinking back tears as he said,

"Dad, I promise you. I will continue staying on the right path."

Ed squeezed his hand. Despite his own drinking problem, Ed had tried to warn Brian over the years of the dangers of drinking on several occasions. But, in spite of all the time I had grieved over Brian's inability to nurture an ongoing relationship with Ed, I chose to see the beauty in their final moments together.

I breathed a deep sigh of relief and gratitude that Brian was able to be with his father. Brian's verbal commitment to his own sobriety on his father's deathbed convinced me that Brian would not turn his back on his word. The door was finally open, but it was too late.

I called Leigh to come back from her job as a schoolteacher. It was time. On her first day back teaching, she had already made arrangements to come before I called. I felt consoled that she had already said her goodbyes the day before.

When she arrived three hours later and walked to her father's bedside, choking back her tears, she said,

"I love you, Dad." She rubbed his arm as she blinked back her tears.

Through cloudy eyes, he whispered in slurred, pressured tones,

"Well, there's my curly blond-haired cutie." He closed his eyes.

Before Ed took his last breath, we all—Jean, his two sisters, their spouses, Leigh Ann, Brian and I—gathered around his bedside, talking with him. Within me, I found the courage to say,

"Go in peace, Ed. You are surrounded by your family, who loves you. I know you tried." My words flowed freely, like water lapping at a distant shore. What was in the past could never be absolved, but forgiveness and healing mattered. I had the sense that he heard the intention behind my thoughts.

CHAPTER 37

Breaking the Cycle, 2017

It's been four years since Brian's last relapse in 2013. I am indeed joyful, but not for one moment do I take his sobriety for granted or even project outcomes very far ahead. His sobriety is his business, and, although it impacts me, I have learned over the years that I have no control over what happens.

Every day, I remind myself to keep track of my own recovery from co-dependency and enabling behaviors.

During Christmas of 2016, Brian and I traveled to Corning to visit my family. Days before our trip, I began worrying again about how Brian would handle being around alcohol, at my brother's house. *What if the access to alcohol re-triggered his drinking?* Old patterns. After much internal debate, I decided there was no choice but to confront him with my feelings. In the past, I would have kept it to myself, but on that day, I resolved not to hang on to my perceived fears. I needed to step out and verbalize my feelings.

"Brian, I have to share a concern," I said, my heart pounding.

As I stood at the kitchen sink after breakfast just a few hours before our departure for Corning, I found myself overwhelmed with anxiety, slipping into old patterns of worrying about things I couldn't control.

"Sure, Mom. What's up?" The buoyancy in Brian's voice was reassuring. He was more open than I was expecting him to be.

"I hope you won't get upset, but are you ready to handle being around alcohol and watching others drink at Uncle Gary's house?"

"Mom," he said. "It's okay you are asking me. I understand. It won't be a problem."

And it turned out I didn't have any cause for concern.

My mind was at ease, and I enjoyed the family time for three wonderful days. During this visit, I realized how the mother in me, yet again, wanted to take upon herself the responsibility of protecting Brian when he was perfectly capable of taking care of himself. In addressing my inner turmoil about our visit prior to our family getaway, I met my own needs so we could enjoy our time together.

The reality is, however, that addiction is always there, waiting in the trenches to steal your loved one away. It's a family disease that affects everyone involved. It is by the grace of God and the sheer day-to-day struggle that the addict can live on his or her terms and loved ones can ultimately find peace and serenity. But this, as I would learn, is not a given.

Today, I am very proud of my son for how far he has come on his own in the past twenty-seven years. In just as many years, I have not given up hope in him while allowing myself to let go from controlling his behavior. Each lesson has been hard-earned.

Although we don't see each other very often, we stay in close contact through phone calls and texting.

It is a joy to have my son back in my life. The hope in my heart that wouldn't ever go away has manifested itself in the capable, compassionate, responsible man he has become.

As Brian maintains his sobriety, one day at a time, he and his sister Leigh Ann now have reunited as sister and brother. As an added bonus, he is now fully present to my two grandsons, who have the joy of sharing their uncle's love and sense of humor.

It's now August 2017, and I am attending a writing conference in New York City. Since I started home peritoneal dialysis in March of 2016 due to kidney failure as a result of cancer chemotherapy, Leigh Ann has offered to drive me and my carload of required equipment and supplies two hundred miles from Amsterdam to Midtown Manhattan. She stayed with a college friend in Brooklyn and planned to pick me up three days later on Sunday.

I am thrilled to be traveling back to the city to see Brian, now employed almost two years by a commercial plumbing company. We planned to meet for dinner on Saturday, the last night of the conference.

As planned, he met me in the lobby of the hotel where the conference was taking place. This time, I didn't worry if he would show up, although it has taken four painstaking years to trust in his sobriety.

As I entered the lobby, my tall and striking son reached his arms out to greet me. There he was, the son I always knew was there—decked out in navy blue dress slacks and a crisp, white dress shirt opened at the collar. All my anguished prayers for his sobriety were now answered in this one, booming reunion.

Together, we attended the five-thirty evening Mass at St Patrick's Cathedral and lit a candle at St. Jude's Shrine, otherwise known the Patron Saint of the Impossible. It was there that I prayed for Brian's continued sobriety and my continued healing and growth.

Afterwards, we meandered through midtown Manhattan until we settled on a seafood restaurant on Eighth Avenue. Over an appetizer of guacamole and chips, I broached the subject of my memoir. Brian had read the latest draft, and I had been waiting eagerly for his feedback. He knew I would not publish it without his approval.

"So, B, what are your thoughts about our story?"

"There are just a few areas I wondered about."

"Such as . . ."

"Well, I don't have it in front of me, but off the top of my head, just a minor detail—you said I was six-two and I'm six-one."

"Easy enough to correct," I said.

"I can't think of any other areas right now, but I will review it again and let you know."

"Are you sure?" I responded, still uncertain about his response. "Bottom line. I need to know if you are okay with me publishing this story."

"Mom," he said, looking directly at me. "Absolutely. I thought you knew that."

I tilted my head and squinted my eyes, incredulous at his response. But what else had I expected of him? I had to start projecting positive thoughts about Brian's responses.

"Yes, Mom. If you had asked me a few years ago, my answer would have been different. But I have accepted that the past is part of who I am today. It's OK."

Relief washed over me, and I exhaled, slow and steady. Brian's acceptance of my story was the condition I'd set for publishing it. I sensed all along in the nineteen years of writing this story—his and mine—that his ability to accept it would be a definitive sign of the level of his recovery.

"Brian, I have to tell you something that happened recently. I was at a Little League game when I saw a man walking up the hill with a young girl who I presumed was his daughter. He looked exactly like your dad when I first met him—tall, handsome, rugged. A thick head of brown hair and muscular build."

"Really, Mom? Brian asked, wide-eyed as he leaned forward.

"When I looked at this man with his daughter, I felt an overwhelming sense of sadness for all that your dad missed out on due to his drinking."

We both paused for a moment. Brian broke the silence, saying, "Well, Mom, I've broken the cycle. I pray I can stay sober, one day at a time, for years to come."

I sat in stunned silence for a moment, taking the moment in. All my prayers for Brian's recovery over the last twenty-seven years were now answered . . . I prayed.

"Yes, B, you broke the cycle—one day at a time," I said softly. Brian smiled and nodded his head in agreement.

> *"I am one with the universal woman, strong, proud, and resilient, tested by the storms of time, washed clean by the tide . . . a smooth stone on the shore. Enduring."*
>
> ~ Personal journal entry

EPILOGUE:

From a Mother's Heart, 2017

For as long as I can remember, it has always been my role to mother my children, whether that meant jumping in to fix every little mishap or showing love for their hurts. Eventually, as they grew up, I would need to learn to let go and let my children navigate their lives on their own.

This has been by far, the hardest lesson for me, as a parent, to learn. As a mother of an addicted son, my understanding of mothering was fearfully tested.

I always loved my son Brian but hated what he was doing to himself with his drinking, which time after time left him floundering and me wringing my hands in angst in an endless series of self-defeating activities.

When he was a toddler, I could just pick him up and remove him from a dangerous situation. I could protect him.

But as he grew, he tested my limits. I could not have known that the seven-year-old who screamed, "Look, Ma—no hands" at the top of the pine tree would one day, as a young adult, find himself stranded, homeless, jobless, and utterly alone.

For twenty-three years, I would not understand that I needed to let go of my need to fix what he could and should do for himself. I continued to enable him, which robbed him of his ability to experience self-empowerment.

At the time, I didn't know that letting go did not have to mean giving up, and I held on tightly to my need to control his behavior and my response to it because I thought that was how to show my love—my go-to response to his troubles.

Gradually, over time, I learned—through support groups, prayer, bonding with other mothers of addicts—that it was better to let go and take better care of myself. Dealing with an addicted child is never easy. I would also learn that it would be possible to experience joy and serenity only if I could separate myself from any chaos brought on by my son's addiction.

Addiction is a cunning beast that leaves its victims shattered and confused. It knows the vulnerability of a mother's heart. It knows that a mother will do anything for her child. It wants you, too.

The mother of an addict has to possess a warrior's stance against the addiction. But addiction does not know that a mother will not give up without a fierce fight. She will battle every day and with every ounce of her being. Fighting for her child often means letting go of the need to control. She needs to focus on her own well-being and know that she can still love her child but needs to let go of her need to control her child's life.

Sometimes the outcome is not what you want and the addict you love dies from the addiction, the fear of every mother. Hope was all I had left when I fell into despair in 2008, the year he went missing in New York City during the Christmas season. It behooves parents of addicts everywhere to focus on the need to live one day at a time—to continue loving their child while taking care of themselves.

A Mother-Son reunion in New York City, 2017

To anyone who has endured the terror and heartache of watching their child spiral downward from addiction, my heart goes out to you. It is my greatest wish that my story will offer hope to those dealing with the darkness of addiction and to believe that recovery is also on the horizon.

I am pleased to report that, as of this writing in 2019, Brian remains committed to his sobriety . . . one day at a time.

APPENDIX

My Lessons of Addiction

If you are struggling to stay hopeful while dealing with a loved one's addiction, read on to discover how these sixteen lessons, based on twenty-three years of dealing with the addiction of my child, can arm you with support for dealing with addiction and to remind you of what you can and cannot control.

I am no expert in addiction, but my personal struggle dealing with Brian's addiction taught me the importance of loving my child and never giving up hope. When love isn't enough, hope steps in.

1. When love isn't enough, open your heart to hope.

2. Everyone's story is unique, and yet there are similarities, no matter the circumstances.

   Even though your son's or daughter's addiction may not be as extreme as others', it can still trigger terror, hopelessness, helplessness, sadness, rage, and fear. In my case, Brian could have been dead at any number of points throughout his active addiction. And I could have been taken down by it all, too.

3. Remember that addiction is a disease, not a moral failing. It is not your fault that your child is an addict.
4. Know that addiction does not discriminate.
5. When the person you love is an addict, s/he is physically alive, but as long as the addiction prevails, the person is mentally and emotionally gone.
6. Differentiate the disease from the person. Hate the disease, but love the addict.
7. Abstaining from alcohol or the drug of choice is the only cure.
8. Understand that there is nothing you can do to force an addict to take responsibility for treatment. You can support him/her in their efforts toward recovery, but it is ultimately his/her decision to seek treatment for their disease.
9. Love an addict, but without the drama of trying to fix him/her.
10. Understand that, to deal effectively with addiction, you cannot deny the problem. My denial interfered with and delayed my son's ability to recover. Denying stalls recovery. Get the help you need to break through the denial.

11. To let go does not mean giving up.
12. Loving a child, though very important, is not enough when it comes to dealing with addiction.
13. Stay hopeful, even when love is not enough.
14. Take care of yourself by setting healthy boundaries.
15. Arm yourself with the knowledge you need to deal with addiction by seeking information and emotional and social support.
16. Embrace the support community, such as Al-Anon. It will be your lifeline as you struggle to understand the disease of addiction and accept your role in addiction.

Selected Resources for Parents of Addicted Children

Arming yourself with information about addiction and how it impacts your loved one will help you understand its dynamics and provide you with a lifelong plan to deal with it.

Online Resources

The National Institute on Drug Abuse:
https://www.drugabuse.gov

Al-Anon:
http://www.al-anon.org

Alcoholics Anonymous:
http://www.alcoholics-anonymous.org

Narcotics Anonymous:
http://na.org

Partnership for a Drug-Free America:
http://www.drugfree.org

Hazelden:
http://hazelden.org

National Association for Children of Alcoholics (NACoA): *http://www.nacoa.org*

Cathy Taughinbaugh, parent coach who specializes in working with parents of children struggling with substance abuse:
https://www.recovery.org/pro/author/cathy-taughinbaugh/
https://cathytaughinbaugh.com/

Selected Memoirs about Addicted Children:

Burwell, D'Anne. *Saving Jake: When Addiction Hits Home.* FocusUp Books. 2015

Cataldi, Libby. *Stay Close: A Mother's Story of Her Son's Addiction.* New York: St. Martin's Press, 2009

Hall, Pattie Welk. *A Mother's Dance: One Step Back, Two Steps Forward, Full Circle.* WriteLife Publishing. 2015

McGuire, Meg. *Blinded by Hope: My Journey Through My Son's Bipolar Illness and Addiction.* California: She Writes Press. 2017

Moyers, William Cope, with Katherine Ketcham. *Broken: My Story of Addiction and Redemption.* New York: Viking Penguin. 2006

Romero, Maggie C. *A Mother's Story: Angie Doesn't Live Here Anymore.* Mercury Heartlink. 2014

Scheff, David. *Beautiful Boy: A Father's Journey Through His Son's Addiction.* New York: Houghton Mifflin Company. 2008

Swenson, Sandra. *The Joey Song: A Mother's Story of Her Son's Addiction.* Nevada: Central Recovery Press. 2014

Resources on Meditation:

Swenson, Sandra. *Tending Dandelions: Honest Meditations for Mothers With Addicted Children.* United States: Hazelden Publishing. 2017

Book Discussion Questions:

1. Although Kathy, as an educated and highly skilled nurse, was well aware that her children were predisposed to addiction due to their father's alcoholism, the forces of her denial seemed to take over. What was your reaction to her response? If you were in this situation, what would you have done differently?
2. Hope is a powerful force when dealing with addiction, and yet it led to "magical thinking" by clouding Kathy's judgment of reality. What role do you think hope plays in coping with the addicted child?
3. Kathy attempted to set limits for Brian by drafting a contract that set abstinence as a precondition for participation in sports, but this proved unsuccessful. How can parents of addicts, especially of growing teenagers, discipline their loved ones effectively?
4. One of the dilemmas Kathy experienced as a single parent of two children was not having the consistent support of her children's father. How do single

parents find the support to consistently deal with an addicted child?

5. Sometimes, other life crises occur in addition to dealing with an addicted child. How is it possible to deal with multiple life crises? What resources have helped you to deal with them?

6. Kathy shares that the life-threatening cancer diagnosis paled in comparison to watching her son spiral into addiction. Why do you think a mother might feel that way?

7. Guilt and shame seemed to underlie Kathy's response to Brian's addiction, which led to her enabling behaviors. What is the difference between enabling and helping behaviors?

8. Education and awareness about addiction as a disease is essential to recovery for both the parent and the child. What were some of the ways Kathy changed her ways when it came to dealing with Brian's drinking?

9. Addiction is a family disease. How was Brian's sister, Leigh Ann, affected by her brother's addiction? What did she do to help herself and her struggling family?

10. Did this memoir shed any new light on the topic of addiction and its impact on family members? If so, how?

Share the Hope

Please help us spread the message of hope to parents of children struggling with addiction everywhere. When I was dealing with the early stages of my son's addiction, I felt alone and scared. Providing support in the form of information and resources can make a big difference to families. Here are some ways to help:

1. Your feedback on Amazon or your favorite online bookseller can help others find the book. Please locate *Just the Way He Walked: A Mother's Story of Hope and Healing* on Amazon, and leave a short review. If you've already registered with Amazon, this will take a few minutes. If you haven't, registration is quick and easy.

2. Please leave feedback and reviews of the book on GoodReads.com and anywhere you are active.

3. We can all do things to make a difference in someone's life. Please consider suggesting this book to a friend, colleague, healthcare providers who work with parents of addicted children, including social workers, family physicians, nurse practitioners,

book clubs, community support groups, church groups, and nonprofit organizations working with the addicted population.

4. Is a copy of *Just the Way He Walked* in your local library? Please consider donating a copy, or suggest that the librarian add it to their collection. Ask your friends and families to do the same.

5. Encourage your local independent bookstore to carry this book.

6. Ask your local newspaper or radio program to review *Just The Way He Walked* or interview the author.

7. Host a book-signing, online event, or speaking engagement to groups about issues related to addiction.

8. The electronic version of *Just the Way He Walked* is available for eBook readers through Amazon or other eBook retailers.

9. Lend your copy to a friend in need.

About the Author

Kathleen Pooler is a retired family nurse practitioner and author of the memoir *Ever Faithful to His Lead: My Journey Away From Emotional Abuse*, published on July 28, 2014, and sequel, *Just the Way He Walked: A Mother's Story of Hope and Healing*. She writes about how she tapped into her faith in God during her biggest obstacles and disappointments to transform and heal from life's greatest challenges. She believes that every little bit of hope matters and that we are all strengthened and enlightened when sharing our stories.

Memoirist Kathleen Pooler

She lives with her husband Wayne in eastern New York and blogs weekly at her Memoir Writer's Journey blog: *http://krpooler.com*

Where to Find Kathy

Twitter @kathypooler
https://twitter.com/KathyPooler

LinkedIn: Kathleen Pooler: *https://www.linkedin.com/pub/kathleen-pooler/16/a95/20a*

Goodreads: *https://www.goodreads.com/user/show/4812560-kathleen-pooler*

Facebook:
Personal page, Kathy Pooler: *https://www.facebook.com/kathleen.pooler*

Author page: Kathleen Pooler/Memoir Writer's Journey: *https://www.facebook.com/memoirwritersjourney*

Pinterest (*http://www.pinterest.com/krpooler/*)

Stories by Kathy Pooler

"The Stone on the Shore" in the anthology: *The Woman I've Become: 37 Women Share Their Journeys From Toxic Relationships to Self-Empowerment,* published by Pat LaPointe, 2012.

"Choices and Chances" in the *My Gutsy Story Anthology,* by Sonia Marsh, September, 2013.

CPSIA information can be obtained
at www.ICGtesting.com
Printed in the USA
BVHW030211010420
576549BV00001B/216